let the heart speak

reflections by
NOMI BACHAR

outskirts
press

Let the Heart Speak
Reflections by Nomi Bachar
All Rights Reserved.
Copyright © 2017 Nomi Bachar
v4.0

The opinions expressed in this manuscript are solely the opinions of the author and do not represent the opinions or thoughts of the publisher. The author has represented and warranted full ownership and/or legal right to publish all the materials in this book.

This book may not be reproduced, transmitted, or stored in whole or in part by any means, including graphic, electronic, or mechanical without the express written consent of the publisher except in the case of brief quotations embodied in critical articles and reviews.

Outskirts Press, Inc.
http://www.outskirtspress.com

ISBN: 978-1-4787-8378-7

Cover Photo © 2017 Nomi Bachar. All rights reserved - used with permission.

Outskirts Press and the "OP" logo are trademarks belonging to Outskirts Press, Inc.

PRINTED IN THE UNITED STATES OF AMERICA

Table of Contents

Acknowledgments i
Introduction iii

Love And Lust 1
One Marriage, Two Souls 2
From Lust To Love 3
A Note On Sex 4
What Acupuncture Taught Me About Love 5
Love: What's Beyond The Feeling 7
Communicating With The Ones You Love 9

Self Love 13
Self-Love Rehab: Step I 14
Self-Love Rehab: Step II – Treat Yourself The Way
    You Would Treat A Precious Friend Or Lover 16
Self-Love Rehab: Step III – Establish Loving Dialogue With Yourself .. 18
Self-Love Rehab: Step IV – Free Yourself And The Rest Will Follow 20
Self-Love Rehab: Step V – Weathering The Storm 22
Self-Love Rehab: Step VI – Violence: A Look Within Yourself 24
Self-Love Rehab: Step VII – Take Yourself On Fun Dates 26
Step VIII-Being Authentic 28
Self-Love Rehab Step IX: Living Like You Are Going To Die 30
Self-Love Rehab-Step X: The Treasure Chest Of The Soul 32

Seasons & Celebrations 35
Living In The Tent 36
Let's Welcome Adar: The Month Of Joy 37
7 Gifts You Can Give To The World 39
7 Gifts We Are All Given 41
Thanksgiving: The True Stuffing 44
Rosh Hoshanah: The Cycle Of Soul Renewal 45
Autumn: Death And Renewal 47
Realigning Your Soul / Realigning Your World 48

Your Inner Shrine 50
Spring: Transformations In Nature And Ourselves 51
Beauty, Transformation, And Death 53
Fireworks And Your Inner Independence 54
Passover And Easter: A Journey Toward Liberation 56
Death And Rebirth 57
Gratitude And Thanksgiving 58
A New Year, A Renewed You:
    How To Create Inner Balance & Harmony 59
Moving From Limitations To Expansion 63
Thanksgiving Being Grateful For The Losses And The Blessings 65
A New Year Of Gratitude 66
Welcome To The New Year! 67

Between Light & Darkness 69
Election Night Torture 70
"Refugee Crisis" – Time To Embrace 71
The Anger In Our Hearts 73
The Future: Are We Building Or Destroying? 75
Gifts And Losses: Giving Thanks 77
Navigating A Troubled World 78
5 Qualities Of A True Leader 79
Peace And War 81
Make A Difference! 82
A Child And A Terrorist 84
Love And Destruction 86
Kidnapping: A Hole In The Soul 88
Lack Of Awareness: The Cost 90
Love And Shooting 92
Hurricane Sandy: Gaining Knowledge From Tragedy 93
Living In A Disconnected World 95
Mutual Responsibility 97
Inspiration In A World Of Bad News 98
The Inner Paradigm 100

Journey To Bliss 103
I Am Of The Earth 104
Passion For Integrity: Lessons From My Cleaning Lady 105
Beginners Guide To An Ease Of Being.. 106
Free Your Energy Field.. 108
How The Eagle Lost Its Beak 110
Take A Vacation 112
Have You Ever Wanted To Fly? 113
The Power Of Choice 115
On Prayer 117
Am I Going To Be Here The Next Moment? 119
Joy In The Journey 120
Tips On Growing Your Blissipline 121
A Fight For Freedom 123
Death In The Middle Of Life 125
The Seeds Of Your Soul 127
The Biology Of Feeling 130
The Man On 23rd Street 132
How To Transform Pain Into Compassion 133
Life Under The Snow 135
About Kabbalah: The Path Of Receptivity 136
Thinking Is Not Living... 138
Opening Our Emotional Center 140
Why Are We Here? 142
Being A Powerful Communicator... 144
Generate Your Joy 145
Freeing The Emotional Self... 147
Suffering: The Hidden Gift 150
An Invitation To Be 152
Resolution: Restoring Flow 155
How Is Your Blissipline Doing? 157
Committed To Grace 159
The You Behind Yourself... 161
Are You On Your Life Path? 163

Your Life Is A Contribution 165
Being In The Moment 167
Transparency And Your Life 169
Ask Yourself The 4 Grand Questions 170
What Is The Universe Made Of? 172
Lack Of Awareness: The Cost 173
Seven Ways To Thank Your Body 174
Your Daily Dose Of Happiness 176
Healthy Pleasures 178
Your Partners, Your Team, Your Life 180
Communication Is Key 182
Live In The Moment 184
Silence And Meditation: Resting Your Mind 185
Living Creatively 187
The Three Gifts 189
The Origin Of Stress 191
A Loving Good-Bye To Whitney Houston 193
Loving Communications: The Ten Commandments 195
The Manifestation Highway 197
Mastering Success 200
A Note On Self Love: Small Steps To Rehab 201
The Importance Of Inner Dialogue 203
Cultivating Your Personal Relationships 205
Life As A Dialogue 207
Use Your Emotions As A Form Of Contribution 209
Our Emotional Journey 210
Celebrate Your Feelings! 211
The Body: A Prison Or A Fire Chariot? 213
Freeing The Expression Of The Body 215
Use Your Body To Tap Into Emotions In Your Daily Life 217
The Gate Of Emotions 219
Getting To Know Our Emotional Self 220
The Inner Map 224
A Note On Nurturing 225

The Wounded Heart 226
The Power Jog! Try This! 227

Magic And Miracles 229
Creating Magic 230
You Create The Miracles 232
Halloween-Soul Magic 234
Co-Creating Your Reality 236
The Power Of Intention 238
On Creativity 239
Shivaratri: Constructive Destruction 241
What Matters? 243
Naked Trees, Unity, And Hope 244
A Violin Out Of Trash 246
Winning The Inner Oscar 247
Healing: How Does It Happen? 248
Express Your Feelings By Using The Arts 249
About The Author & The Gates Of Power ® Program 251

Acknowledgments

I am grateful to all of you, loved ones and friends. Your love and support have sustained me through the many ups and downs. To all you who have been reading my writing, you have inspired me to keep going by expressing your thoughts and feelings to me. Most of all, I am grateful for the spirit of love and creativity that keeps pouring into my life.

Introduction

This book is a collection of blogs and essays that I've written over the last few years. They're just heart reflections that come to me spontaneously in different moments. I would like you, the reader, to find that freedom. Write whatever pours out of your heart as you read each entry. Take your time with this book and allow the subjects, thoughts, and concepts to resonate with you while making connections into your own life. I have provided small spaces for you to record your thoughts as you read (though, you are certainly not confined to that space).

Some themes weave themselves back and forth in this book. They should be treated just like refrains in a musical piece.

Enjoy reading and let your heart speak.

Love and Lust

One Marriage, Two Souls

Marriage is a sacred assignment.

Two souls come together to realize more of their true selves. Marriage partners bring up in each other all that is unresolved, making way for emotional and energetic imprints to come to the surface in the presence of love. The partners will challenge, inspire and support each other. When honesty and dedication to growth are the partners' common ground, the two will face their inner pain and fears together, and at the same time, discover their highest capabilities. They will be each other's best friend, yet uncover their strength and center as individuals.

True marriage is a real soul purifier. All that we need to let go of, shows up within intimate relationship with our partners. And all that is possible, amazing and unconditional is available. It is up to us to walk the path of true transformation that the gift of marriage offers us.

WRITING REFLECTION

_____

_____

_____

From Lust To Love

Osho is one of my favorite spiritual teachers. I would like to use this medium to share his thoughts with you regarding lust and love.

He wisely says that when you become interested in a woman or a man as an object, sooner or later the interest is finished because once you have explored the object, nothing is left. Then you are ready to move to somebody else. The woman looks beautiful, but how long can she be beautiful? An object is an object. She is not yet a person to you; she is just a beautiful object. It is insulting. You are reducing a soul into an object, a subjectivity into an object. You are trying to exploit. You are turning her into a means. Your energy remains ignorant, and you go on moving from one woman to another; your energy is running in circles.

He says, love means you are not interested in the woman or the man as an object. In fact, you are not there to exploit the other; you are not there to get something from the other. On the contrary, you are so full of energy; you would like to give some energy to the person. Love gives.

And when love gives, it remains subjective, it remains rooted in oneself. Lovers help each other to be more and more themselves. Lovers help each other to become authentically individual. Lovers help each other to be centered. Love is respect, reverence, worship. It is not exploitation. Love is understanding. Because energy is unoccupied with the object, it remains free, untethered. And that brings the transformation.

WRITING REFLECTION

_____

_____

_____

A Note On Sex

Somewhere along the way, we lose the ability to just be alive, while we enjoy our moments and the experience and adventure they provide. Sex is one of these wonderful experiences we receive when we are open to life and willing to be fully alive.

Instead, we use sex to "get" love and collect admiration and attention. We use it as a relaxation pill, a sleeping aid, a punishing or manipulating strategy, a way of controlling another, etc. The pure pleasure of giving and receiving enjoyment and affection is lost all because we don't truly and deeply accept and love ourselves.

I remember myself as a young, insecure woman collecting admirers and using my sex appeal to get a sense of value. My true appreciation of others and life came about as I was learning to accept and appreciate myself. Only then, did I discover sex and intimate exchange to be an adventure in openness, an experience of freedom and flow, a dialogue of pleasure, energy, and joy.

Keep letting go (it happens in stages) of all that is binding your authentic expression and genuine appreciation of yourself.

WRITING REFLECTION

_____

_____

_____

What Acupuncture Taught Me About Love

What would happen if all of us, each one separately and altogether, could beam love? Powerful, warm, compassionate, accepting beams of love that would radiate from within ourselves surround us, and travel beyond. Beams of love would melt and release our hostility and our sense of separation, fears, and anger. Does it sound like a children's story or a corny fantasy? I say it is worth trying.

My acupuncturist is a small, thin man who has been clearing the energy pathways of his clients for close to 30 years. When he works on you, he becomes a passionate channel of the universal intent to flow and expand. While sticking the needles everywhere in his patient's body, he mumbles lovingly: "Relax, release, let go, let it be, you are the flow."...

I don't necessarily enjoy the needles, but my heart bathes in a warm smile listening to his loving mumbles. The hardened places within us, born of fear and pain, need to dissolve, and love is the greatest dissolver of all that is not life affirming. On my acupuncturist table, I am reminded of the healing power of love. He loves his clients, and that love is expressed in his commitment to clearing their chi, their life force.

He makes me think of all the love that surrounds me. Do you stop for a minute to acknowledge the love that surrounds you in your life? The honest concern of friends, the kindness of neighbors, the casual help of strangers, the warmth of loved ones, and so on.

Acknowledging and enjoying the love around me has become a very important practice. Since I counsel people, I naturally feel the love and affection in me toward my clients on a daily basis, but noticing and accepting the loving energy I receive from others is just as important as well. The exchange of love- giving and receiving is the most nurturing and fulfilling element of life. It gets lost in the endless torrents of to-do lists, survival chores, social and economic obligations. I have made it a priority in my life to notice this exchange. I refuse to let it drop to the bottom of the list. What about you?

WRITING REFLECTION

_____

_____

_____

Love: What's Beyond The Feeling?

Is it enough to feel loved or it is not love unless it is expressed in actions? Shouldn't the feeling of love affect and impact positively the person who is loved?

I am reminded of a great love I had in my 20s. We were both "crazy" about each other. He would write me love notes and leave them all throughout the house. His poetry journal was filled with poems about his love for me. It was all beguiling and flattering, but his actions did not match the passion of his words and feelings. He was always late for dates. He did not think that it was a big deal if he said that he would call at seven and call three hours later. He would almost always be very busy when I needed practical help, and the list goes on. Okay, he was young and inexperienced with being in a loving relationship. I was too, and I am sure that I frustrated him out of my ignorance and anxiety.

Unfortunately, this type of behavior and even much more destructive in some cases is not only a characteristic of youth. We have to admit that people of all ages make the same mistake of not matching their love feelings with their love actions. If your loved one does not feel nurtured, respected, and considered, check your love actions. They are somehow not registering as loving in your loved one's heart.

Loving feelings are wonderful, but we all must learn to match them with loving actions. True love looks for ways to enhance the emotional and physical well-being of another, to support their desires, needs and dreams. If we are not enhancing a loved one in a tangible, consistent manner, our love feelings are like seeds, but are not bearing fruit. Love is powerful; it can save a loved one's life, literally, emotionally or spiritually. As we mature the more, we hopefully learn to find ways to impact each other positively and generously.

LET THE HEART SPEAK

What is happening in your love life beyond the gifts, the chocolates, the dinner, etc.

WRITING REFLECTION

_____

_____

_____

Communicating With The Ones You Love

Love is undoubtedly the most life-giving, transforming and inspiring experience within the realm of existence. When asked, most people would put love on top of their list of most important elements. Family and being connected with our loved ones give us a profound sense of fulfillment and meaning. When we are honest with ourselves, in the silent moments, we recognize that life without loving relationships is empty, cold, and desert-like. No matter how successful we are in our career, no matter how financially affluent we are, well traveled or socially recognized; our hearts will not be truly joyous or fulfilled without love.

The simple daily interactions with the people that care about us, keep us going. The love that we feel and express towards others generates an inner energy in us; thus, inspiring us to create and expand. Love is truly the motivating force behind all creation and its healing ability manifests in all aspects of life.

So why is it that we are not able to communicate constructively with the people we love most? The answer is simple. The experience of love can be divided into two elements: the inner emotion of love, and the ability to actually express it. Many times we feel the love, but we don't have the tools and the practice to articulate the feeling in a way that would enhance the connection. Communication skills need to be learned and practiced. Meanwhile, since we're not receiving this training as part of our 'education', we need to do everything possible to acquire these skills ourselves.

If you want your life to be rich, enjoyable and passionate; you need to cultivate your relationships. Investing in positive and loving relationships yields the highest emotional return.

One of the most important elements in cultivating loving relationships is communication. Most of us struggle with finding our emotional voice. Sometimes, it's because we are scared to speak from our heart, or we don't know what the heart wants. Other times, we get stuck in our pride and defensiveness.

The keys to communication are simple as long as we remember to use them. Below are some tips derived from my **10 Commandments for Successful Communication**[1]:

1. **Commit to creating connections.** Take responsibility for the success of your communications. Be the cause, the initiator, the giver.

2. **Cultivate empathic listening.** Extend that to listening to yourself and others. Empathy helps you understand and accept. It enhances transformation and change.

3. **Avoid reactivity.** When faced with strong emotions and intense reactions, take a minute to figure yourself out. Get clear and strive to create a constructive way to communicate.

4. **Learn to negotiate.** Create win-win situations. It is best for all those involved.

5. **Show appreciation.** Do whatever you can to validate your loved ones. Use listening and mirroring skills, show respect and consideration. You can still maintain your beliefs and stand up for them. One has nothing to do with the other

---

[1] "10 Commandments for Successful Communication." Let the Heart Speak. *"Journey to Bliss."*

COMMUNICATING WITH THE ONES YOU LOVE

Communication is an art. Keep experimenting and go through the trials and tribulations. Not only will your loved ones enjoy it, but you will enjoy it as well. And, isn't that the goal – to be happy, open and expressive?

WRITING REFLECTION

_____

_____

_____

Self Love

Self-Love Rehab: Step I

This section, we begin our self-love rehabilitation. In the next nine sections, we will walk through ten steps that will strengthen your connection to yourself, and deepen your self-love and self-appreciation.

The first thought I would like to introduce to you is the power of choice. In every moment of life, you make choices, whether you're conscious of a present decision or not. You must train yourself to be the master of your choices. You can't leave them to chance. You can't leave them to others. You can't blame them on your childhood, your spouse, your boss, or any other person or circumstance.

At the root of our global economic woes, for instance, is a decision to leave things to chance and play the blame game. And just as economies appear to be collapsing under a weight of inaction and indecision, so too will the marketplace of our heart and soul if left without a commitment to bold decision making and actions. The simple fact is that it is all up to us. We have been given the free will to choose and create our lives according to our vision. And we need to embrace this gift. By making conscious, constructive, creative choices, we gain dominion over our lives.

Are you ready to make choices that will lead you to self-love? If you are, here's the first step: Make a list of at least ten things that you like about yourself. The list can include your gifts, skills, character traits, physical attributes, etc. Choose to accept your embarrassment, insecurities, or even guilt, and go ahead, have a ball appreciating yourself.

When I give this assignment to my clients, a lot of them immediately feel uncomfortable. This happens mostly because we are not taught to appreciate ourselves. It is considered selfish. So we shy away from appreciating the things we like the most. And if we have to make a list of those things we like about ourselves and declare it to others, we feel embarrassed, or at the very least, awkward. You too might experience all these feelings, and here is where the word "choice," comes into the picture. Make the choice. Do it now. Your tendency might be to postpone this. But just make the choice.

WRITING REFLECTION

_____

_____

_____

Self-Love Rehab: Step II – Treat Yourself The Way You Would Treat A Precious Friend Or Lover

Daily, we identify with our body, our personality, our temperament, our possessions, and we need to keep reminding ourselves that within the house of our familiar self, resides "The Self." A spark of the great creative force, the universal consciousness lives within us, expressing itself through us. It guides us, protects us, and provides for us. When you treasure and love yourself, you are honoring and loving that divine spark, which is the center of your being.

Loving yourself means loving The Self. As you walk through your day, remain aware of how you treat yourself. Begin to inquire about your habits and daily routine. Start with simple things:

- How do you greet each new day? What loving, simple actions do you take to nurture yourself in the morning? Do you stare into the mirror and criticize yourself? Or do you find yourself worthy of appreciation?

- When you're making yourself breakfast, do you consult lovingly with yourself on what would be nurturing and appropriate to consume each morning? Do you take time to enjoy your food, which by extension means enjoying time with yourself? When you pour your bowl of cereal or make your toast, do you serve it to yourself with a smile? Or do you just swallow it in one helping as you rush off to do life's bidding?

- When you're selecting your wardrobe for the day, do you consider what will add joy to your day, or make you feel fun and flirty, or do you simply contemplate how others will perceive your look?

SELF-LOVE REHAB: STEP II – TREAT YOURSELF THE WAY YOU WOULD TREAT A PRECIOUS FRIEND OR LOVER

- Throughout the course of the day, do you create the time to ask yourself, "How do I feel?" "What's going on?" as you would inquire of a spouse, child, or friend?

- Do you take moments through your busy day to enjoy the sky, someone's smile, a child at play – the little gifts of life that offer inspiration?

- At the end of a day, do you create the time to relax, laugh, share a story with loved ones, listen to their tales, meditate, sit silently, or write down thoughts?

The tasks of self-inquiry that I've asked you to commit to are all tiny acts of love towards oneself. Devotion is love in action. And when you are devoted to your true being, you are devoted to life,to others, and to the Creator. So, please create a little time and be devoted to yourself – today.

WRITING REFLECTION

_____

_____

_____

Self-Love Rehab: Step III – Establish Loving Dialogue With Yourself

In "Self-Love Rehab: Step 1," we reviewed the power of "choice." In "Self-Love Rehab: Step 2," I emphasized the idea that the universal and loving intelligence lives within us.

In "Self-Love Rehab: Step 3," we will uncover how whatever you feel, think, and do, affects –believe it or not – our dynamic global ecosystem. Maybe you think this sounds a bit grandiose, or even unbelievable, but think about it this way: **How many times have you stepped into a meeting with a chip on your shoulder,** and somehow, the entire atmosphere shifted from one of excitement and joyous buzz to that of sullen blandness?

My point is this: Whether you do or don't love yourself, your attitude causes a ripple effect in the universal emotional realm. And to be generous and care for yourself, first is to be generous and caring for the rest of humanity.

To love someone properly, you need to know them – know what they need. Know what they appreciate and desire. When you have a basis from which to reach out, you can meet their emotional needs as a supportive friend and loved one.

We will consider steps that will help you become that trusted friend to yourself:

1. Make time – say, 15 – 20 minutes – to complete this exercise.

2. Take two sheets of paper and place them opposite each other, one on your right and one on your left.

3. On the paper to your right, jot down the question: "What is it that I need to feel loved, fulfilled, and joyful?"

4. Now, on the same sheet of paper, proceed to elaborate on the question above. Encourage yourself to write down everything, just like a good parent would encourage their child. Doing this will help to uncover some of the scenarios that serve as a roadblock to your happiness. *For example, you may write to yourself: "I know that you've been very stressed at work lately. What are you feeling? Are you afraid? Angry? Hurt? How can we remedy these negative feelings so that you can proceed healthily and happily?"*

5. Now move to the second page, and write in big, bold letters: **"These are the things I need to feel, do and know in order to feel better…"**

6. Then, from your deepest, emotional core respond freely and from your heart. List everything that you need to feel happier.

7. Once completed, acknowledge these needs. Choose a couple of actions that will address them. *For example, if you need to talk to your boss to resolve an issue, devise a plan, and do it.*

Once you follow up with loving actions to support your needs, you will begin to sense a seed of inner strength growing. You are becoming that beautiful, proud tree you were designed to be.

WRITING REFLECTION

___

___

___

Self-Love Rehab: Step IV – Free Yourself And The Rest Will Follow

What is the magic of forgiveness?
When we hold a grudge; harbor resentment; or cling to bitter anger or judgment, our whole body, mind, and soul collectively experiences it.

Everything that we think or feel registers within our being. Lack of forgiveness harms us gravely.

The magic of forgiveness is its power to dispel dark clouds from within our consciousness, its ability to free our whole being.

On the other hand, just wanting to forgive doesn't make it happen.
We all have witnessed, for example, a peace agreement on paper that has failed to become a reality in everyday life. Forgiveness is a process that starts with the intention and desire to let go of bitterness and broaden compassion. And, while we're talking about peace processes, for that matter, having the intention to forgive is the first step in forgiveness. Individual forgiveness is the first step needed to achieve global peace. The remaining steps should follow.

I have spoken to clients who have declared that they have forgiven their parents or siblings; but, as their emotional work unfolds, we find that bitterness is still there, and it is unfairly projected onto others.

Wanting to forgive and actually forgiving are two separate things.
Sometimes, it takes a while to truly forgive. First, we need to feel the anger, sadness, and bitterness that block our forgiveness.

SELF-LOVE REHAB: STEP IV – FREE YOURSELF AND THE REST WILL FOLLOW

Acknowledging these feelings and processing them constructively helps us achieve forgiveness.

1. Choose three incidents in which you are unable to release anger or offer forgiveness.

2. Select a person connected to one of these incidents and list all the feelings that surface when thinking of that person and incident.

3. Acknowledge the hurt underlying your lack of forgiveness. Here's where you give yourself the love and understanding to empathize with yourself and appreciate your feelings.

4. Consider what you would say, if given the opportunity, to the person who hurt you, from a place of authentic vulnerability. Jot down your statement as if you were face to face with that person.

5. And finally, consider the other person's point of view for doing or saying whatever it was that hurt you.

If you follow these initial guidelines, you will be well on your way to true forgiveness. There are more steps in this process, but this is a great place to start.

WRITING REFLECTION

_____

_____

_____

Self-Love Rehab: Step V – Weathering The Storm

One day, after a big storm, I was walking in the park and was struck by the vision of broken and uprooted trees. I was wondering why is it that some trees break apart while others get totally uprooted, but yet many seem to be robust enough to weather the storm. **I thought of myself and other people in my life and wondered what helps us weather the storms of life?**

When it comes to trees, I know that well-grounded, deep and strong roots help a tree survive a storm. **People are like trees; we need strong roots to ground us into the soil of life, and help us withstand our personal storms.** Most of us are going through political, social and personal storms that challenge us. All over the world, we are witnessing people being uprooted from their homes and lives threatened by terrorists and violence. **The question is how do we develop strong spiritual and emotional roots that are solidly grounded in life?**

The first thing that comes to my mind is living a life of contribution. To live such a life, we need a deep desire and a focused intention to be of service, and actions done out of love. A mother devotes herself to her child. She is spiritually and emotionally interested in her child's well-being. That devotion and contribution ground her in life. We have all seen women transform when they become mothers. Imagine how your life would be if you had the same devotion, passion, and intention to contribute **to your loved ones, to your community,** and **to yourself.**

What are you dedicated to that helps you cultivate these deep roots in life?

WRITING REFLECTION

f-Love Rehab: Step VI – Violence: A Look Within Yourself

Every day while watching the news, we encounter violence. I frequently ask myself what makes people, nations, and groups violent.

Groups are made of individuals. Each one of us can contribute to either violence or peace. These contributions can be very subtle; every thought, word, or small action can elicit anger or joy. I would like you to take an honest look at yourself and ask yourself the question: what causes me to feel violent?

This kind of honest self-examination needs to become a daily awareness. It is necessary to cultivate the understanding of what causes us to react violently. By saying that, I don't mean an outward attack, such as hitting someone or throwing something. I mean a violent feeling within.

I found that when I feel victimized by somebody (that somebody could be me) or something, a fit of anger surfaces. I dedicated many years of my life to eradicating a sense of victimization. What empowered me to move away from the victim state of mind was taking full responsibility for everything I create in my life. Establishing myself as the creator rather than the victim shifts me out of anger into loving action and constructive communication.

It is extremely empowering to stand in the position of being the cause and the generator of your life. Look at situations in your life in which you feel at the mercy of or the effect of "powers" outside of yourself. Meditate on the ways that you participate in the situations that are unhealthy or upsetting for you. Ask yourself how you contribute to the circumstances of your life. What can you do to shift your ways of being, doing, and communicating so that you can establish yourself in a place of conscious choice, integrity, and responsibility. This equals inner peace.

WRITING REFLECTION

_____

_____

_____

Self-Love Rehab: Step VII – Take Yourself On Fun Dates

How many times do you take yourself, just you and yourself, on a fun date? Most of the time, we think of fun dates with other people, friends, siblings, mates, children; we associate fun with being with others. It's the same mistake we make when we think of receiving love, support, or compassion. We associate these with the generosity of other people. In reality, we need to be the first ones to be generous with ourselves.

It is important to learn to give ourselves the compassion and advice we need and become self-reliant, while still welcoming support from our friends. The same applies to having fun. How liberating and wonderful it can feel if you can take yourself on fun dates and enjoy them thoroughly even though it's just you. Doing this is necessary; it's a part of learning to be your best friend, to be your loving parent, and to be your playmate. I would recommend taking yourself on a fun date at least once a week. Dates don't have to be over planned, extravagant affairs. They can be simple such as:

- Sitting on a park bench and watching the sky, the trees, the people, relaxing and just having a good time, taking a moment out of your busy day and taking in the world.

- Doing something small, like renting an old movie you love and want to see again.

- It could be making some new and exotic food that you have decided to put together for yourself as an experiment.

- Going on a bike ride and visiting a part of your neighborhood that you have not visited for a long time or checking out an interesting museum exhibition

SELF-LOVE REHAB: STEP VII – TAKE YOURSELF ON FUN DATES

- For the more adventurous, you can try taking yourself on an extreme adventure like hang-gliding.

The idea here is to cultivate a habit of having fun all by yourself. When you can be your best friend, you will find out that you are so much more relaxed in the relationships you have with others. Once you are at ease, you will not go into relationships with acute needs that may burden the other person. You will have become your primary caretaker, and you will enjoy and honor this role.

Some may consider having fun to be frivolous or self-indulgent. It may even elicit feelings of guilt – why should I be out having fun when so many others in the world are suffering? Unfortunately, this is a limited perspective that isn't accurate. We cannot underestimate the powerful effect that healthy, constructive fun can have on diffusing stress in our lives. By choosing to create fun in your life, even on a very small scale, you may have a larger effect than what you may consciously realize. You can never quite know the impact your lighthearted spirit and actions will have on the lives of others.

Go ahead and discover the pleasures of being your playmate.

WRITING REFLECTION

_____

_____

_____

Self-Love Rehab: Step VIII-Being Authentic

Authenticity is not encouraged in a society that is addicted to image. Striving to look good is the opposite of being authentic. Unfortunately, our culture and media focus on projecting an image, an image that has nothing to do with the truth of one's being. This trend encourages an addiction to celebrities. We look for false idols to follow and imitate at the cost of our personal authenticity. From skinny jeans to Venetian shades, we are like lambs led to the pasture of "trends."

Loving yourself is not about falling in love with your façade. A friend from Twitter asked me to write about the "ego." The ego is the part of ourselves I define as the "Defensive Self." The Defensive Self is that part of us which is concerned with survival and safety. It is attached to an outside source seeking for recognition, validation, and reassurance. This aspect of ourselves is formed at a young age; at a time we look to secure love at any cost. To get this attention, some of us become addicted to excelling, others become rebels, and yet many become pleasers. These are just some of the ways we skew ourselves to get love, attention and a sense of safety.

If you are reading this book and you are an adult, part of becoming emotionally mature is to learning to be self-reliant regarding recognition, validation, and reassurance. However, this is not to say that we shouldn't be open to enjoying others' support and praise. But those should be in addition to what we already have within ourselves.

Adulthood is the time to look within and find out who we truly are: our vulnerabilities, strengths, needs and desires. It is a time to learn to honor and nurture our authentic essence and find creative and expressive ways to enjoy our truth and share it with others.

Exercise:

Choose one significant relationship in which, you are not allowing yourself to be completely authentic.

Ask yourself:

- **What kind of image am I trying to project in this relationship?**
- **Why am I doing this?**
- **What would I truly like to express if I was not withholding my truth?**
- **Am I willing to take a risk and share who truly I am?**

If you've done the exercise and are ready and willing to take the risk and be more honest –**GO FOR IT!**

When you are honest, you inspire more honesty, and honesty leads to transformation.

WRITING REFLECTION

_____

_____

_____

Self-Love Rehab Step IX: Living Like You Are Going To Die

This section was written in October of 2011 after the passing of Steve Jobs.

The Transient and fragile nature of life glare at us when a loved one gets sick or dies or when we are going through a possible life threatening experience. All of a sudden, the simplest moments of life become precious. Our errands turn into sweet little songs of joy. Colors, textures, people, and nature take on a deeper dimension. Somehow when we are immersed in our daily living routine, we conveniently dim this realization, and rob ourselves from the intense aliveness that is available to us.

One of the ways to love yourself is to gently wake up and remind yourself that you are not here forever, not in this form or in this life. Your soul is eternal, but your current life is transient and precious. Living in the presence of death is a good way to live; maybe the only way to truly appreciate life.

When we don't take life for granted, our love and enjoyment intensifies. More importantly, our connection to the people that we love deepens. Steve Jobs' death hit us with a sense of loss and profound respect for his contribution and dedication to his vision. His death coincided with the ten days of awe leading to Yom Kippur, which are, according to the Jewish tradition, days of soul searching, and realignment with our highest ideals and vision.

You are invited to live awakened to this amazing opportunity that is life: An opportunity to realize and contribute the best in you. You are here to add your unique choreography to the existing universal

SELF-LOVE REHAB STEP IX: LIVING LIKE YOU ARE GOING TO DIE

dance. No matter how small or offbeat your steps are; they still leave a mark.

WRITING REFLECTION

_____

_____

_____

Self-Love Rehab-Step X: The Treasure Chest Of The Soul

This section was written in October of 2011 during the Occupy Wall Street Protests.

Life is a journey and a quest. There are always challenges and obstacles around every corner. I see the news and realize the impact of negativity on the world. Yet it is inspiring to see people fighting the good fight such as the Occupy Wall Street protest. How do you fight the good fight without it wearing down on your spirit? Nourish yourself by filling up the treasure chest of your soul. Keeping a smile on the face of your soul can keep you afloat when the waves of life are crushing on your shore. How do we fill up the treasure chest of our soul? Here are some tips to keep our soul happy.

- **Great Memories:** Enjoy your moments and internalize their beauty. When you are in the midst of a moving moment crying, laughing, loving or meditating. Open your heart and your consciousness. Record the moment internally, and store the 'DVD' in the treasure chest of your soul. A library of great memories is a source of joy; you can revisit and relive.

- **Magic Moments:** At the end of the day, choose one magic moment. It can be as simple as a glimpse of the sky, playing with a dog, or giggling with your mate. Acknowledge it, savor it, and store it away in your treasure chest.

- **Victories**: At the end of the day, acknowledge one big or small victory. For example, saying no when it is definitely what you want to say or saying yes to something that frightens you. Add your victories to your treasure chest

- **Gratitude:** During your day, take a moment to stop, close your

SELF-LOVE REHAB-STEP X: THE TREASURE CHEST OF THE SOUL

eyes and think of three things for which you are truly grateful for. Add those to your treasure chest.

Keep filling up your soul's treasure chest with inspiring, heartwarming, funny, and lovely goodies. All of us are warriors of good. Our treasure chest can never be too full because there is always more good times ahead.

WRITING REFLECTION

_____

_____

_____

Seasons & Celebrations

Living In The Tent

On a Sunday, I was at a public art event in Peekskill. One of the installations was a group of fifteen small tents crocheted by hand. The little tents beamed with vibrant, powerful colors and at the same time looked fragile. Feelings of sadness and hope rushed through me. The little camp of tents reminded me of all the thousands and possibly millions of us who at one point or another did not have a home and had to live in a tenuous structure supported only by our hope, faith, and trust in the benevolent nature of life. (The countless migrants are experiencing this right now).

So many times in my own life I was "living in a tent," which to me meant living through a hard period filled with unknowns, questions, doubts, and fears. Moments in my life where I felt like I was sinking into the quick sands of existence. During these times, I was forced to reach out to a power greater than myself, even when I was not convinced at all there was one.

I was humbled and helpless enough to allow my heart to open and receive. These frightening periods of my life ended up being my most inspiring. It was during these times I found my connection to the Spirit.

The Jewish holiday of Sukkot in which Jews create little structures made of wood brush and curtains for walls, comes to remind us of the tenuous nature of our earthly life and at the same time the infinite source of support available to us by Spirit. All we need is an open heart.

WRITING REFLECTION

_____

_____

_____

Let's Welcome Adar: The Month Of Joy

Yesterday, sitting in a Kabbalah lesson, I was struck by an idea that was presented by the teacher, Rabbi David Ingber. He talked about the meaning of the Jewish month of Adar (רָדָא,). I always looked forward to Adar as a child. My siblings and I used to have competitions as to how many sweets we could eat throughout the duration of the month, for as the Jewish saying goes, "When Adar enters, we indulge in joy." The month proudly hosts the holiday of Purim. It is a playful time of masks, costumes, and goodies, in which you are instructed to get drunk.

So what is the deep meaning of all of this?

I thought that joy and fun were good enough, but lo and behold, yesterday, I discovered a most comforting and insightful meaning associated with this month. The letter א in the Hebrew spelling of the month of Adar (רָדָא,) represents the unity of all creation, and the way it is channeled and maintained through us human beings. The רָד part of the word means «lives and resides,» in Hebrew.

Our joy in the month of Adar is two-fold. First, it is a release into playfulness and learning how to be lighthearted. However, the deeper reason to indulge in joy is the knowledge that all creation springs from a loving source.

As much as we may get discouraged, horrified, or upset by human cruelty, we have to keep clearing our inner vision and rest in the knowledge that the Presence of the Spirit permeates all creation. It is the only true reality, no matter how hidden it is behind fearful reactions of greed for power, control, and domination.

WRITING REFLECTION

7 Gifts You Can Give To The World

There are seven gifts that we have been given. Without these gifts, we would not have the abundant potential to give to others. **These same seven gifts are the gifts that you can give to others and the world.**

The holiday season offers us the opportunity to pause and meditate on the importance of love, joy, and the exchange of gifts. Doing so, we find a deeper meaning in these most joyful and important elements of life.

It is a joy to know we can pass onto others the gifts we are given.

Here are seven gifts that you can give:

1. **Talents, Abilities, and Passions**
When we express talents, abilities, and the passions we were given, we enrich the lives of those that receive them.

2. **Guidance, Intuition, and Spiritual Sense**
If you allow yourself to be an open channel of intuition and guidance, you can give this gift to others in many different ways. We all need feedback, counseling, spiritual support, etc. As we open up to our intuition, we can encourage others to be open to theirs as well.

3. **Physical Comfort**
We all take physical comfort for granted, but we get many gifts from the natural and physical world. Think of the many ways you give the gift of physical comfort to yourself, loved ones, and others. Here are some examples: creating a garden in your backyard, helping a friend de-clutter, building a shed together, cooking a meal, letting go of things you don't need and offering them to others, or donating money to charity.

4. **Emotional Support and Confidence**
If we let ourselves, we can be loved and supported daily by the people in our lives, the kindness of strangers, the support of our peers and friends, the inspiring, and moving acts of great people all around the world. All you need to do is take all this love and support you receive and pass it on to others.

5. **Knowledge**
The gift of knowledge is available to us 24 hours a day. We can learn about the world around us, not only in class, but also from being present in our lives and open to the wisdom of our elders, peers, and strangers. The gift of knowledge is not complete unless we're willing to share it with others. It gives us great joy to impart knowledge that we have acquired to others, thus, encouraging more learning and more knowledge.

6. **Creativity and Beauty**
Each one of us is endowed with the gift of creativity, and the ability to appreciate beauty and express it. Our uniqueness, originality, and creativity are the ways we move, inspire, and entertain others.

7. **Community**
Creating a community is a gift that we both receive and give at the same time. The community supports us physically, spiritually, and emotionally. Close knit relationships empower and nurture us. Having a community helps us fight depression and illness, slows aging, promotes mental health, and even leads to a longer life.

WRITING REFLECTION

_____

_____

_____

7 Gifts We Are All Given

The holiday season vibrates with the themes of joy, love, giving, and coming together. These themes should be close to our heart all year round. Still, it is good for us to be intensely reminded of them for at least two weeks out of the year. In doing so, we find a deeper, more personal meaning and a greater passion and dedication to express these most joyful and important elements of life. Think of your daily needs. Here they are, categorized from the most basic to the highest:

- Security Needs
- Social Needs
- Physiological Needs
- Cognitive Needs
- Aesthetic Needs
- Self-Actualization
- Spiritual Needs

The most amazing gift is that we can fulfill all these needs. All we need to do is be clear about what they are, be open to receive, and commit to their fulfillment. Isn't it a tremendous blessing that we have within us that we need to fulfill our needs?

Here are seven gifts that you are given:

Notice that they are the same gifts that you can give, as mentioned in the prior section.

1. Talents, Abilities, and Passions
When you were born; you were given talents, abilities, and passions. These lead you if you honor them, to great fulfillment and joy.

2. Guidance, Intuition, and Spiritual Sense

If you take the time to go within, even just a little bit daily, and ask for guidance, consult your intuition, and honor the answers that you get, you are provided with clear navigation on your life path. All you need to do is sit still, ask, and listen.

3. Physical Comfort

We all take them for granted, but we get many gifts from the natural and physical world. Nature provides for us through our tending to it with food, shelter, water, air, and healing. What's more, we are recipients of all the pleasures and conveniences created by us and inspired by nature.

4. Emotional Support and Confidence

If we let ourselves, we can be loved and supported daily by the people in our lives, by the kindness of strangers, by the support of our peers and friends, and by the inspiring and moving acts of great people all around the world.

5. Knowledge

The gift of knowledge is available to us 24 hours a day. We can learn about the world around us not only from the books we read or the classes we take, but also from being present in our lives, and open to the wisdom of our elders, peers, and strangers. Not only do we receive practical tips on the way the world works and how we can improve it, but we also learn how to live spiritually and emotionally.

6. Creativity and Beauty

Each one of us is endowed with the gift of creativity, and with the ability to appreciate beauty and express it. When we "think outside the box," not satisfied with following the crowd, we activate our creativity. The creative mind believes that the best ideas have not yet been thought of. Uniqueness and originality are the ways to achieve personal fulfillment and to create beauty in the world.

7. Community

Being part of a community is a gift. Community supports us physically, spiritually, and emotionally. Close knit relationships empower and nurture us. Having a community helps us fight depression and illness, slows aging, promotes mental health, and even leads to a longer life.

Be open to appreciate all these gifts Life offers you, honor, and be grateful for them. Remind your heart to take a few minutes a day to rejoice.

WRITING REFLECTION

_____

_____

_____

Thanksgiving: The True Stuffing

I love Thanksgiving for many reasons. One, it gives me an opportunity to consciously stop and ask the question "Why am I thankful?" Two, it marks the beginning of the winter season and I can enjoy the weather without suffering too much. Three, I love the colors of Fall, and the colors of the food; the yellows and golds of squash, the deep orange of sweet potatoes, the reds of cranberries mixed with all kinds of greens. Last but not least, the company of loved ones and friends. The laughter and warmth are all things I am grateful for.

WRITING REFLECTION

_____

_____

_____

Rosh Hoshanah: The Cycle Of Soul Renewal

Rosh Hashanah marks the beginning of a ten day purification and re-alignment process. Just like nature is getting ready to shed and move into a renewal pattern, the human soul is getting ready for another cycle of spiritual growth. The soul is yearning to shed old or negative constricting patterns and usher in life affirming insights, positive commitments and new possibilities. Rosh Hashanah honors this natural cycle of the soul. We are given 10 days between the start of the cycle, which is, the Jewish New Year up to Yom Kippur, the Day of Atonement, which is really a day of attunement.

In these ten days, we have the opportunity to engage in an introspective soul searching, a time to forgive and be forgiven, a time to receive and release. These ten days are said to be the most auspicious days to draw closer to the Creator, as well as to reconcile our relationships with ourselves and each other. In the course of the year, we may have hurt others, and we may have been hurt by them. We draw closer to our nature when we open our hearts and our minds to forgiveness. We get ready to renew our commitments to ourselves and our community.

Opening ourselves to this process enables us to receive a higher vibration of the life force energy and blessing. It is said that on Rosh Hashanah, we open up to who we really are and at Yom Kippur, we let go of who we are not. Rosh Hashanah might be likened to the inhalation of the breath bringing in new vitality and Yom Kippur may be likened to the exhalation of same, releasing what is no longer needed and what does not serve us. Both processes are related and intimately connected.

Other traditions honor a similar process. For example, the celebration of Maha Navarati is also a ten day process of letting go of earthly bondage and connecting with the power of Shakti. Whether the cycle of nature calls to your soul or your cultural tradition, I hope you take this time and make it your personal period of inner cleansing and strengthening.

WRITING REFLECTION

_____

_____

_____

Autumn: Death And Renewal

Autumn always reminds me of the necessity of death for the sake of renewal. Have you noticed that just before the leaves die and drop to the ground, the trees are covered by striking colors of gold and red shimmering in the light? I call this the moment of their enlightenment. It is as if the leaves know that they are dying and are bursting with the last drop of life, celebrating their life and their death, both at the same time. I imagine that they feel they will join the earth and live in another form. It seems like nature knows that "death" is necessary to renewal. What we see as death is a just a transformation from one state of existence to another. Maybe this is why I feel autumn is a celebration of letting go, with all the glorious colors and incredible beauty.

We can all learn from nature to trust the little or big "deaths" in our lives, the shedding of the old. If we can let go, we can renew and heal.

I love coaching and assisting people in moving through the past and beyond it. We look at and identify what is true and lasting within us and what is unnecessary, limiting, and false. Being who we truly are is our source of inner strength and success.

WRITING REFLECTION

_____

_____

_____

Realigning Your Soul / Realigning Your World

In Jewish tradition, the 10 days between Rosh Hashanah - the Jewish New Year, and Yom Kippur, the Day of Atonement/attunement, is a time for deep reflection and inner realignment. We all carry within us old habits of stress rooted in fear, negative beliefs, and defensive patterns. These beliefs and patterns shackle our spirit, cripple our aliveness, and clip our wings. This 10 day period is sacred to practicing Jews, as it gives them the opportunity to do a full cleaning of the soul. They get to reinvent, renew, and revive their spirit. Everyone can take this opportunity, as it is also a time of change in nature. The leaves are changing their colors, getting ready to die, and the trees are going into winter hibernation. The process of renewal is clearly upon us.

Look at your life's closets and see what is presently not enhancing or fulfilling you. It is now time to make space for the new patterns. Here are some guidelines according to the Gates of Power® method. Gates of Power® defines 7 portals of being. These are the channels or Gates, through which our being radiates out into the world and vice versa. Ideally, all these channels need to be open and energized for us to feel balanced and whole. The Gates of Power® method assists you in the process of clearing these channels. For today, let's engage in some fall clearing to make space for expansion.

Here are 3 of the 7 Gates- see what you may want to clear up in these 3 areas.

- The First Gate is the **Gate of the Body**- This Gate includes your physical being, as well as all external material structures, such as your home environment, your car, your computer, your finances, etc. Take a minute and choose one thing that you need to release to improve the state of your body or your environment. It could be as small as removing clutter or other nonfunctional objects, or as big as letting go of a negative habit that harms your body. Make a choice to let go of it, taking advantage the steps that are necessary to do so.

- The Second Gate is the **Gate of Emotions**- Choose one emotional habit that doesn't work for you. For example: repressing agitated emotions or holding back on expressing love, etc. Make a decision to let go of it and contemplate creating a positive emotional habit with which you can replace it.

- The Third Gate is the **Gate of Dialogue**-This is the Gate of communication and relationships. These include your relationships with others, as well as yourself. Take a look at your relationships and define a pattern of relating that is not working for you. Examples: harsh self-criticism and/or a tendency to control others. Make a decision to let go of it and meditate on the practical way to support your decision.

WRITING REFLECTION

Your Inner Shrine

On the 4th of July 2014, Ananda Ashram and Yoga Center dedicated the new shrine to the beloved Guru Shri Brahmananda Sarasvati. As I was sitting there in this beautiful space, I was many times moved to tears by the words and feelings shared. I realized that in the Guru's presence, as well as in the presence of my own inner Guru, we can find our inner shrine; a place of total peace, of acceptance of ourselves and others, love and kindness, and an open heart to oneness. The inner shrine is the place we want to take ourselves to every time we meditate or at any moment we can. It reminds us of our true nature, which is love, bliss, and creative power. We are indeed in great need of as many reminders as possible.

Shri Brahmananda Sarasvati created a beautifully accepting grounds; a place where east meets west, arts meet meditation and different spiritual traditions live side by side honoring each other, and exchanging their wisdom. There is a true sense of unity and respect. For the past 15 years, I have lead two of the most important Jewish holidays, Rosh Hashanah and Passover at Ananda Ashram. What other ashram in the world opens its gates with such deep respect for other spiritual traditions? It is that inner shrine of love and accepting all expressions of life that we can create within our hearts, thus, letting its loving warmth permeate our daily existence.

WRITING REFLECTION

_____

_____

_____

Spring: Transformations In Nature And Ourselves

Each year between seasons (and I have been around for many of them) I await with childlike excitement for spring when the magic of nature transforms from the cold winter to the first hints of green. This winter, more than ever, I can't wait to see the emerging buds celebrating their passion for life, waiting to burst with brilliant colors. Did you ever wonder how this magic happens, this total transformation from dull and gray to glorious and beautiful?

The magical transition from winter to spring demonstrates the power of transformation that resides in nature. It takes us from night to day, from hatred to love, and from sickness to health. The same power resides in the soul of each one of us. The soul yearns to shed its suffocating cloaks and claim its brilliance, a state of freedom, joy and creativity. Our defensiveness, fears, pain, and distrust keep us imprisoned. Consciously or unconsciously, we know it. We feel like we're not fully alive or something is missing. We feel an inner emptiness and a sense of loss and in a way that is true.

The fact is that we, ourselves, are the roadblocks to our transformation, a natural process that moves life in constant cycles of evolution. It takes a decision to make a choice, commitment, and discipline to get ourselves unstuck, to undo our self-imposed stagnation. As strange as it might sound, we are attached to our contraption; it feels safe and familiar, even though it is unpleasant. We hold on to our fears and pain because freedom feels dangerous. We long for it and distrust it at the same time.

We also know intuitively, that if we let go of our inner repression, we will begin to experience our emotions at a much deeper level.

Our feelings might come out gushing. We are terrified of the intensity of our emotions. At one point in my life when I was consciously releasing difficult emotions, I remember feeling painfully brittle when sobbing. It felt as if I was shattered into small pieces. I had to find courage and self-acceptance, again and again, to continue the healing process.

Many of us are looking for easy ways to feel good. I did the same in my younger years. We try to find comfort in things, substances, fame, glory, approval, and avoidance. This kind of comfort works for a short time and then we need more different and better. Needless to say, this is a kind of comfort that far from facilitates transformation is the opposite of growth, and ultimately, it is deadening to the spirit and soul. If we want to transform, we need to tolerate what is uncomfortable. We need to take ourselves out of the protective box and claim our aliveness. We need to take risks, open up, and express. Living with a passion for the truth and the courage to discover it connects us to the power of transformation: a power that lives within us, guiding our journey.

WRITING REFLECTION

_____

_____

_____

Beauty, Transformation, And Death

Fall is the perfect time for transformation! All the components of change are in the air! Our bodies are invigorated by the cooler air and change in seasons. Time is shifting, and so is our awareness.

As I walk through the woods, the feeling of the cool, crisp air against my cheeks, the smell of freshly fallen leaves and the comfort of a warm sweater against my skin awaken my senses and remind me of what it feels like to be alive! It is in such moments I am truly experiencing life!

All these wonderful sensations lead me to experience the moment wholly throughout my body. I become fully present and aware of all that I am and all that is around me. I am in the moment. It is in this stillness that I can be grateful for who I am and where I am headed. It is in this moment of utter gratitude that I have the opportunity to be guided in creating the life I want. It is in this moment I remember I am not alone, but closest to all possibilities and things.

In this moment I am in a state of alignment, free, peaceful, and trusting.

WRITING REFLECTION

_____

_____

_____

Fireworks And Your Inner Independence

I was watching the Fourth of July fireworks boldly splashing their colors in the sky. The kid in me, struck by their exquisite shapes and patterns, was "ohh-ing," and "ahh-ing," along with the New York crowd gathered by The Hudson Bay. All of us had turned into children at play, wrapped in a magical moment. I was grateful for being independent, here in the United States, and maybe more importantly, in my heart.

My Expanded Self was filled with a sense of deep gratitude for my personal journey in the United States – a journey filled with challenges and victories. I was experiencing a state of wholeness and inner liberation. Each of our journeys towards an open and expanded state is an ongoing mystery; that unravels deeper layers of insights, discoveries, and realizations.

I have just arrived home after visiting Israel and Ireland. I find that every time I step out of my daily activities and into newness, I am given an opportunity to stretch and uncover a part of myself that may not be awakened in the context of the "regular me."

In this section, I would like to share how I allowed the Irish in me to pop up. Think of your heart as a planetary jigsaw puzzle (your soul as a cosmic one). The pieces of the puzzle include different cultures, countries, vistas, foods, songs, and arts, etc. When you visit a new place, that piece of the puzzle settles within you and your heart has an opportunity to experience it. Ireland, with its majestic and raw nature, peaceful untouched cliffs, meadows, and bays, opened me to the Celtic mystique within. I could imagine myself roaming the fairy lands barefoot, immersed in nature's comfort and bliss.

In my daily life, I eat mainly raw vegan food. I don't drink alcohol or coffee, and you would almost never find me in a pub. In Ireland, I was happy eating potatoes, fish and chips, buttered scones, and brown bread. I was sipping Irish coffee and pints of Guinness – not at all, the "regular me." I sang in pubs, danced, clapped, and was silly. It was wonderful to feel Irish. That is what I mean by inner independence, freeing us from ourselves (even when our self is a very well-balanced whole self). My advice is: always take journeys. They can be two hours long, or two months – just take them, they are liberating.

WRITING REFLECTION

Passover And Easter: A Journey Toward Liberation

Passover and Easter both celebrate the human journey towards liberation. We all yearn to be free socially, politically, economically, emotionally and spiritually. Freedom, life's most cherished gift, is also the hardest to achieve. The Passover story is a powerful metaphor. We are all, to some degree or another, imprisoned by our fears and defensiveness. We become slaves to our cravings, addictions, and insecurities. The good news is that there is a Moses, a spark of the Divine, in each one of us. We are all journeying through a "desert," towards our personal promised land.

The story of Easter is also rooted in the idea of liberation. The resurrection story of Christ, Yeshua of Nazareth, an enlightened spiritual teacher, provides us with a moving lesson. We are called to realize that we are not our body or our carnal mind. We are spiritual beings, eternal and indestructible. Isn't this realization the ultimate freedom?

In the recounting of the Israelites redemption, Moses, on behalf of God, asks the Pharaoh for the people's freedom over and over again. "Let my people go, so that they may worship me." The Torah reminds us that our freedom is directly tied to our responsibility and our mission to create a better world and serve others. This story tells us that our ultimate job is not just to be liberated, but to be liberators.

WRITING REFLECTION

_____

_____

_____

Death And Rebirth

It is the end of 2012, and we are all very much still here. The doomsday prophets and the ascension light workers are all alive and well. What do we do now? It seems like we need to keep creating, maintaining and transforming life, very much the same way, we humans have done for many cycles. Nothing in the three-dimensional universe stands still; when a cycle ends, a new cycle begins. What has always been true is the power and responsibility we have to choose our actions and creations. Life givers and life killers always have the chance to come together, dissolve duality and inspire new patterns and new possibilities.

How about you personally? What are you going to create in the next cycle? What are you passionate about? What is most important to you? In this window of time, imagine that you are being handed, by your Expanded Self, all angles and spirit helpers, a magic wand, and with it, you are given the right and the responsibility to create more beauty and goodness. You can spread the gold-dust of your soul around and transcend people and plant life, just a little more joining the love forces in their eternal dance. Take the wand and command a wish. You have that power in your hand, now and always.

WRITING REFLECTION

_____

_____

_____

Gratitude And Thanksgiving

Gratitude is giving thanks for everything in our lives. Giving thanks for the small things can lead to bigger things. When we give thanks we open ourselves up to the gifts of the universe. The universe responds and gives us more. It is similar to when you smile at a stranger and they smile back. The positive vibes not only affect you, but affect others as well. This Thanksgiving, give thanks for the things you have, the things you don't have, and for the things yet to come.

WRITING REFLECTION

_____

_____

_____

A New Year, A Renewed You: How To Create Inner Balance & Harmony

A new year is a wake-up call, infused with a sweet invitation from destiny to take the next step up. Ideally, we should have the habit of examining our lives weekly, asking the questions: What works, what doesn't, why, and what is needed? But most of us are not as diligent as we should be.

The New Year will flash a sign of "Stop and Think," in front of our eyes and whisper: "The clock of time keeps ticking away silently; you will not be here, in this version of yourself, forever. It is time to take stock of your life and yourself." I invite you to take a minute and ask yourself: "What area of my life is clearly out of balance and needs more attention right now?"

- Is it your family?
- Your creative projects?
- Your health?
- Your spiritual evolution?
- Your emotional freedom?
- Your finances?

Write down your answer on a sheet of paper. This is the item highest on your priority list. The one you are most passionate about. The second question to ask yourself is: "How committed am I to creating a new level of possibilities in this area?" If your commitment is wavering, the third question is: "What's standing in the way?"

LET THE HEART SPEAK

Strong emotional commitment is the key to manifestation. Actualized desires spring from our inner being. "As within, so without." If you want love, you need to be love. If you want health, you need to envision health, etc. To achieve growth and balance in the area of your life that you chose, you need to nurture your whole being. All aspects of our lives are closely connected. Your state of being is the soil in which all dreams grow and blossom, and you are the gardener. Make sure you provide a fertile soil for your inner being if you want your dreams and wishes to come true.

Our inner being expresses itself through seven channels. I call these channels The Seven Gates of Power®. When all seven channels are open unblocked, expressive, energized, and working together in harmony, you are a whole, powerful, and expressive being. You then enter into a state of being that supports the manifestation of your visions and desires.

Imagine yourself as a flower with seven petals. All petals have to be nourished and opened for the flower to express its beauty fully. In the same way, all of your Gates need to be nourished, cleared and energized in order for your inner light to shine.

The Seven Gates of our being are:

- The Gate of The Body (also includes all physical structures of life, home, care, and finances)

- The Gate of Emotions

- The Gate of Dialogue (relationships with yourself and others)

- The Gate of Creative Expression (adventure, playful and creative projects)

- The Gate of Life Path (your life's purpose and direction)

- The Gate of Silence (prayer and meditation)
- The Gate of Knowledge (learning)

If you neglect any one of these Gates, you compromise your inner balance. All the Gates are connected and work together in synergy. Here are some tips for creating wholeness in preparation for the New Year:

1. Take an honest look at each one of the Gates and ask yourself what you need to strengthen and cultivate in this area of your life.
2. Make three clear commitments relating to each Gate. For example, the Gate of the Body: How do you intend to strengthen your body in this coming year? Nutrition? Exercise? Rest? Grooming? Or, the Gate of Emotion: How can you create greater emotional freedom and connect with feelings you are avoiding? Express your feelings more, better, differently? Learn to understand or accept certain emotions?

Once you finish going through this process and you have made three commitments under each Gate, you are ready to chart your plan for renewal and empowerment.

I suggest that you create a colorful chart with seven columns and three commitments under each column. Now that you are clear about your commitments, it is time for practice. You will need to consult your chart on a daily basis to create small steps leading to the accomplishment of your commitments.

If you are making a bold move out of your comfort zone, and I hope you do, be prepared to encounter fears, self-doubts, and resistance. This is the natural process of growing. There are always breakdowns, small and large, before breakthroughs. Keep working consistently through these.

LET THE HEART SPEAK

It is a sacred labor of self-love; the rewards of your efforts will deepen your understanding of yourself and your ability to nurture and empower that self. It is your creative gift to yourself for the New Year.

I wish you a year of health, joy, and renewal.

WRITING REFLECTION

_____

_____

_____

Moving From Limitations To Expansion

For us to materialize our desires, it is not enough to say we want something. What's even more striking is that it is not enough to feel the want. Achieving what we desire depends on our emotional availability to receive it. If you have negative beliefs about your self-worth, you will question whether you deserve to receive; you will have doubts about your right or your ability to achieve. You might have a fear of failure or a fear of success. You might distrust yourself or others. All of these beliefs will end up sabotaging your process of achieving and receiving. Many of us end up in a state of despair and frustration when we don't seem to achieve what we want over and over again. We must become aware of the negative emotional beliefs operating within our consciousness and as a result, our subconscious mind. We need to take time to examine and eventually release these beliefs. At the same time, we need to plant the seeds of life-affirming perspectives and keep reinforcing them. This process of realigning is one of the most important gifts you can give yourself.

Take a minute to examine the area of your life that you choose to bring to the next level. Ask yourself:

How am I preventing myself from manifesting what I want here?

What are the patterns of thinking, feeling, and doing that are not working for me?

Why am I holding on to these patterns?

What is the payoff (the seeming advantage) I receive by staying attached to my limiting beliefs, and what has it cost?

What will I need to let go of and give up to free myself?

What new ways of thinking, feeling, and doing can I envision for this area of my life?

What am I willing to commit to and act upon to manifest what I want?

We have old defensive ways of being that worked for us in the past because they helped us survive, but they are confining us now. Gently, without self-judgment or blame, take a good look at yourself. The New Year is a good moment to face up and make a shift. You deserve to be happy, healthy and accomplished.

WRITING REFLECTION

_____

_____

_____

Thanksgiving Being Grateful For The Losses And The Blessings

A good friend of mine lost her daughter this Friday to an illness. Losing your child is the most devastating loss. How does a parent learn to accept that kind of a loss? How do they continue living with a gaping hole in their life and their soul? There is no easy answer to this question.

We all experience losses continuously, small losses and tragic ones: loss of a job, loss of a loved one, loss of a tooth, loss of youth, loss of a home, and loss of a cherished dream.

Can we learn to feel grateful in spite of continual losses? Can we learn to accept what life takes away, as well as what it blesses us with? Can we grow through both experiences? We can, and we have too. Everything we are faced with can inspire us to attain a deeper understanding and a sweeter appreciation of life, its preciousness and its magic.

I invite you to meditate on and write down three painful losses consciously, and three gifts life has brought your way this year. Can you find a reason to be grateful for the losses and the blessings?

WRITING REFLECTION

_____

_____

_____

A New Year Of Gratitude

"Let us rise up and be thankful, for if we didn't learn a lot today, at least we learned a little, and if we didn't learn a little, at least we didn't get sick, and if we got sick, at least we didn't die; so, let us all be thankful." –Buddha

Before this year ends, take time to meditate on all things for which you are grateful for.

When we are grateful, we acknowledge the universe's loving generosity manifesting in our lives.

When we are grateful, we affirm our connection and oneness with the universe's love.

When we are grateful, our hearts feel a deep trust in divine order and goodness.

When we are grateful, we touch bliss and know happiness.

"Let's be grateful for those who give us happiness; they are the charming gardeners who make our soul bloom." - Marcel Proust

WRITING REFLECTION

_____

_____

_____

Welcome To The New Year!

The holidays celebrate the passing year and usher in the new one. It is a special time that marks renewal. We let go of the old and invite in new possibilities. Take time to evaluate the year that is ending—sweet memories, challenges, victories, and unfinished projects. As you say goodbye to the year that ends, acknowledge yourself for everything you have done, emotions you experienced, relationships that you deepened and good times that will remain in your memory. Think of all the new things you have learned and all the challenges you bravely faced. After you take it all in, breath and proceed with the exciting job of creating the next year of your life!

Creating and planning your new year can be overwhelming. Your life has many facets; your mind, your body, relationships and your career, are all examples. Gates of Power® is designed to energize the seven facets of your life holistically. (Read more about all the Gates of Power at http://www.gatesofpower.com/method.htm)

Gates of Power® defines seven areas of life: the Gate of the Body, the Gate of Emotions, the Gate of Dialogue, the Gate of Creative Expression, the Gate of Life Path, the Gate of Silence, and the Gate of Knowledge. Each one of the Gates addresses the personal and the broader area of life connected to that Gate.

I will introduce each of the Gates to you. Each of the seven facets may open your eyes to a new way of thinking about your life.

The first Gate is the Gate of the Body. This is a particularly interesting Gate, to begin with, as it relates closely to how our feelings and actions during the time of the New Year. For example, you are probably already thinking about all the calories you will be consuming over the holidays, the sex, drugs and rock & roll you might indulge in, or the aftermath of self-loathing you might find yourself wallowing in.

When you are finished engaging in one or all of these year-end traditions, and you are ready to start anew, Gates of Power® will be standing by with a word of advice.

WRITING REFLECTION

_____

_____

_____

Between Light & Darkness

Election Night Torture

This section was written in November 2016 in response to the results of the United States Presidential Election which Donald Trump won.

The other night was a sleepless night for many. Turning in our beds or sofas, we were waiting with baited breath for the verdict. Who was going to impact our lives for the next four years? We have been disillusioned, grossly watching the two leaders act in ways that, to me, were totally unacceptable. Different styles of unacceptable acts, but unsettling nonetheless. What is that telling us about the state of our nation? Our leaders are an expression of us, and in turn, they influence our state of affairs, as well as the social and political fabric of the country.

We chose a president who has expressed negative opinions about women, Mexicans, Muslims, other leaders, sexual orientation, and so on. Now, he speaks about unity, a word that has been used as a token bribe by both leaders. "Unity and peace are not the norms," said a friend. Yes, they're not. They take tremendous honesty, integrity, real caring, and spiritual maturity to even to touch the hem of their garment. It takes daily work and commitment. What are our leaders committed to other than their personal ambition? I wish I knew. I would love to be able to look into the heart of that commitment beyond the words, the posturing, and the political maneuvering.

I am, and I know we all are longing for a leader who truly cares about people. All people, all kinds of people. Where is that person? Will we see a tinge of that in the next year?

WRITING REFLECTION

_____

_____

_____

"Refugee Crisis" – Time To Embrace

This section was written in September of 2015, in response to the refugee crisis and an image of a boy on a beach that went viral.

A Syrian toddler, dead on a Turkish beach after the boat in which his family was attempting to flee to Europe capsized at sea. Desperate families crowded a Hungarian train station, their children slept on floors and sidewalks, fearing Hungary will keep them in sinister-sounding "camps." Greek tourism towns were filled with tents and humanitarian workers to accommodate the refugees that arrived daily at the shores in rickety boats.

Isn't it time to realize that we are one human family, forever interrelated, interconnected, and fiercely interdependent? The current "refugee crisis" is a global, painful scream that cannot be ignored. It splashes the obvious in our face. We are one people!!! Whatever happens anywhere happens everywhere. This planet is not divided into separate puzzle pieces. Even though we conveniently still want to see it this way. We no longer can. The realization that we are all impacted by anything that happens; no matter how remote is the bold writing on humanity's wall. We are called to shift our perspective.

This time of soul renewal, marked by Rosh Hashanah, is an opportunity to shake off some more of the inner separation tightropes constricting our heart, mind, and soul. I personally welcome this moment in time to further free myself from any residues of fear, distrust, and contraction so I can experience an even deeper union with all of life.

LET THE HEART SPEAK

WRITING REFLECTION

_____

_____

_____

The Anger In Our Hearts

This section was written in April of 2015, in response to the riots and violence in Baltimore.

The recent violence in Baltimore is another disturbing incident in a string of violent and frightening tragedies. It casts a light on the many in our society that are angry and emotionally lost. Anger turned into destructive violence is slowly but surely poisoning our culture and ourselves slowly but surely. Violence such as this often comes from a place of rage and hopelessness. It's frightening to see that it is happening more and more frequently. What is our society learning from these tragedies? Acting out of anger only temporarily solves the issue. Anger is a natural feeling; what matters is what we do with it. How do we react and what do we create?

It takes the strength of character, a solid moral and emotional compass, and a love for self and others not to fall into the pit of bitterness, anger, resentment, or resignation. Many of us buckle underneath what looks like senseless cruelty, extremism, and brutality that laces our lives and filters into our homes, minds, and souls. We lash out in regressive ways due to our failure to regulate our emotions.

How do we stay positive, loving, and committed to doing good? It is a moment-to-moment struggle, a continuous commitment to choose to live on the side of peace and compassion and act from there. The Baltimore Riots showed us how a group of people affected by a long history of oppression and brutality lashed out in violence, causing further destruction and unsettlement. This will create a never-ending cycle of hate that will only lead to more lives being lost.

How can we settle society's minds and souls in the realm of peace? I don't know an easy answer, and it is not an easy task.

LET THE HEART SPEAK

We need to look in the mirror long and hard. Crises are a call for change, and this one is a very thunderous scream. Make it your business to become part of the necessary and inevitable shift. Use your love and your passion to manifest the message of compassion for yourself and humanity. That message to me is an invitation to give birth to an expanded consciousness within ourselves—experiencing one's self as one with all people and all creation.

WRITING REFLECTION

_____

_____

_____

The Future: Are We Building Or Destroying?

The two holidays that we celebrate this month, Chanukah and Christmas, honor the dominion of spirit within matter. In the story of Chanukah, a handful of Jewish warriors were able to defeat an enormous Greek/Roman army. Their victory stems from their passion, belief, and connection with the spiritual. In the story of Christmas, we're celebrating the birth of a spiritual master whose message is love and oneness with the Father, which to me means oneness with the universal consciousness. Both traditions celebrate the ability of us humans to unite and work with spirit world.

The times we live in are violent and turbulent. We can observe two extremes within humanity's consciousness and manifestation. On the one hand: greed, commercialism, and materialism are accelerating. The source of this phenomenon is a disconnection with self and others, and inner emotional and spiritual hunger. On the other hand: healing and unity consciousness is gathering momentum and with it the flowering of teachers, scientists and light workers who are the vehicle of transformation, and the wave of the future.

Many of us are caught in the in-between, the gray space that is neither this nor that. It is time to take a stand as to which camp we belong. Are we going to be the takers/users, or the givers/creators? We all have some gray shades or undecided little corners, but we are called to make choices in our personal and collective life to create the present and the future. It looks like we must wake up, gradually or not so gradually, and align ourselves with the forces of constructive creativity.

I try to take an honest look at my choices and actions on a daily basis, and I would like to invite you to do the same. There are two ancient questions that human beings have asked since the beginning of time. These can help us stir ourselves in the right direction. The questions are: who am I? And, why am I here? If you ponder these deeply and sincerely, you will keep unraveling the layers and reach interesting insights about your true nature, your gifts, and your lessons. This inner quest will put you in the camp of the builders and creators who are committed to shaping the future.

WRITING REFLECTION

_____

_____

_____

Gifts And Losses: Giving Thanks

Last night, as I was watching the news cycle through its newest tragedy, be it ISIS, Ebola, or the Israeli-Palestinian conflict, I thought to myself that we are a culture fascinated with loss. With every passing tragedy, we forget that our lives are a balance of joy and suffering. Our tragedy-based culture sees gifts as something fleeting that we do not trust and losses as a hard fact of life.

Our fascination with death leaves us with emptiness in life. But how could we possibly know death if we do not seek it in the heart of life? Life is fashioned from the losses and gifts that we are given; each shapes our souls and makes us whole. For loss and gain are one, even as the river and sea are one.

We all experience losses continuously, small losses and tragic ones: loss of a job, loss of love, loss of a tooth, loss of youth, loss of a home, and loss of a cherished dream. Can we learn to feel grateful in spite of continual losses? Can we learn to accept what life takes away, as well as what it blesses us with? Can we grow through both experiences? We can, and we have too. Everything we are faced with can inspire us to attain a deeper understanding and sweeter appreciation of life, its' preciousness, and its magic.

This Thanksgiving, I invite you to consciously meditate on and write down three painful losses and three gifts life has brought your way this year. Can you find a reason to be grateful for the losses and the blessings?

WRITING REFLECTION

_____

_____

_____

Navigating A Troubled World

In the midst of greed destroying the environment, the sabotage of personal and social freedoms, political strife, a life overwhelmed by media and the internet, as well as the basic struggle to survive economically, individuals must do something. In the privacy of their souls, they must cling to their right and obligation to make choices that are constructive and loving. What an arduous task!

It takes the strength of character, a solid moral and emotional compass, a passion for life, as well as a love for self and others to not fall into the pit of bitterness, anger, blame, resentment, or resignation. So many of us buckle underneath what looks like senseless cruelty, extremism, and brutality that laces our lives and filters into our homes, minds, and souls.

How do we stay positive, loving, and committed to doing good? It is a continuous challenge and commitment to choose and act on the side of forgiveness and compassion. Watching the news, there are many parts of the world that are being devastated by political/social forces, natural disasters, disease, and economic strife. To me, the brutal condition in Syria is a symbol of our struggle to maintain human dignity intact.

Are we able to settle our minds and souls in the realm of justice, unity, and love? Not an easy choice. If we can awaken to this truth, we can find our inner peace.

WRITING REFLECTION

_____

_____

_____

5 Qualities Of A True Leader

For many months now, we have been the audience to the uninspiring banter of our two presidential candidates. We all discussed the issues, we got angry, we debated among ourselves, at times we got hopeful, and at other times we despaired. I must admit that I felt discouraged and at times disgusted by the lack of true leadership conduct exhibited, particularly by Donald Trump. It prompted me to think about the qualities of a true leader and the two words that came to mind were "servant" and "leader". I know a story that highlights my point.

Centuries ago, during the Revolutionary War, a group of soldiers were trying to move a heavy piece of lumber that was blocking the road. As hard as they tried, over and over again, they couldn't seem to move it from the ground. Their corporal stood nearby giving them directions and probably graciously allowing them a brief period of rest. He may have even sought their input on "how" best to move the huge piece of wood. But after their repeated efforts, his patience was wearing thin.

Another more senior army officer came along on horseback and observed their efforts. After a moment, he suggested that the corporal help his men. The corporal responded with a tinge of offense in his voice, "Me? Why? I'm a corporal sir!"

The senior officer dismounted his horse and stepped over to the men. He positioned himself alongside them, and gave the order to "heave." All of a sudden, the timber moved into the position where they needed it, no longer blocking the pathway.

He then turned to the corporal and told him, "The next time you have a piece of timber for your men to move, just call the commander-in-chief." The officer was George Washington.

Washington's behavior modeled servant leadership. He led by example. He didn't merely direct others, or solicit their input. He demonstrated his willingness to serve and support them. And as a result, the soldiers felt his tangible encouragement of their work, and he understood the challenges of their roles.

To be a servant leader means aligning the passion in your heart, the vision in your head, and the actions of your hands. Qualities of a true leader include:

1. Deep care and passion expressed in your contribution to your community.
2. Knowledge of your purpose and capabilities.
3. Taking full responsibility for your vision.
4. Doing what you do best and delegating to others according to their skills and abilities.
5. Evaluating daily whether you are proceeding in alignment with your mission.

Each one of us is a servant leader in this life. We serve the people, the projects, and the missions we are involved in and we lead our life according to our vision with a sense of passion and responsibility. I feel that these qualities are the minimum we should ask from the leaders of our country.

WRITING REFLECTION

_____

_____

_____

Peace And War

So many places in the world right now are affected by the tragic impact of war. It feels like a wave of hatred is enveloping the planet. Each one of us can contribute to the healing of this wound by committing to peace. Peace in the simplest, most trivial moments of life and peace as a way of living; a daily practice, meditation. It is not an easy path because tensions, deadlines and life's trials challenge our inner peace. Just as it is true with any deed we undertake, peace needs to be committed to as a daily practice of thought, feeling, and action.

What is in the heart of man that fuels hatred and revenge?

What is in the heart of man that keeps him/her from forgiving, letting go and allowing peace to reign?

What is it that keeps us defensive, distrusting and angry?

What keeps us feeling victimized and in need of victimizing?

WRITING REFLECTION

_____

_____

_____

Make A Difference!

Watching the news in the last couple of days has been disturbing. Thousands of immigrant children are pouring across the nation's southern border from Central America to enter the United States. These children's families are trying to provide them with a better life by sending them to the US in hopes of fleeing the poverty, crime, and drugs-filled communities into which they were born. These children are left alone, vulnerable, and without their families at a crucial development point in their young lives. It is heartbreaking. I have to admit that throughout the last few years, the news has been consistently troubling. It seems as if we have lost the right direction as species. Where are we going, or better still, where are we taking ourselves?

We have created a tremendous ecological and environmental imbalance, and we're paying a very high price for it. We are creating a social, political, and economic imbalance. Why and how did it happen? The answer is a lack of regard for the earth and our human family. Greed and a culture of addictive consumerism driven by materialism have brought us here. Even though the writing is on the wall, a lot of us are in denial, going on our merry way of acquiring, abusing and hoarding more and more.

It seems like we're making decisions without consulting our soul's wisdom and guidance. We're following our physical and emotional desires, most of which are based on a sense of lack and fear.

Let's contemplate the three levels of being: the Spirit, the Soul, and the Personality. The Spirit is the divine spark which emanates and gives life to everything in the universe. It is the loving fabric of all that exists. All individual souls are directly connected to One Spirit. Each one of us can receive guidance insight and wisdom from it if we choose to. The personality is made of our Emotional Self and Defensive Self.

These two parts of us should be guided by our Expanded Self and not vice versa. Our soul encompasses all three aspects.

The actions of greed, destruction, and corruption happen when people are not consulting their soul's wisdom. When we operate from negative desires and impulses, driven by our defensive and emotional limitations, we destroy not create. We are not isolated beings; we are all connected and interwoven with each other. If some of us are being destructive, we are all affected.

Take a minute to look at your life, the decisions, and choices you make. What is driving you? Is it your Expanded Self or is it your defensive desire to look good or gain status and power? Are you coming from love or are you busy controlling and manipulating? Are you living like you are one with others or are you immersed in your needs and desires without considering others? We all have a way to go to become more attuned with the right direction. The first step is admitting to ourselves when we are off course and committing to our innate desire to create love and contribute.

WRITING REFLECTION

_____

_____

_____

A Child And A Terrorist

Last night, I had a deep conversation with a good friend of mine who is also a counselor and a psychotherapist. We were both heavy hearted about the overload of negative and destructive events that seem to be overshadowing society's creative and loving influences. It feels like the battle between darkness and light is extremely obvious, and we are standing at a pivotal point. How can we, regular people, who are doing our best to contribute to society, have an impact on the balance between destruction and construction? Since we are one mind and energy, each one of us does impact consciousness and energy with the way we exist, feeling, thinking, and acting.

My friend and I ended the conversation, reinforcing the belief that what we can do is hold on to the love and light that is within us and continue to spread it through our counseling work with others. It seemed very humble and maybe it is just a drop in the ocean, but we both realized that just by doing that – holding on to the light and not being dragged into the destructive melodramas – we are taking a stand for life. If a four-year-old child can make a difference, having an impact on a terrorist by nature of his innocence and truth, we can all be, if we choose to, agents of light.

If you haven't read it, here is the story as reported by the UK's news agency The Independent:

A four-year-old British boy survived the Kenya shopping mall attack after telling an armed jihadist, "You're a bad man," according to the boy's uncle who granted an interview to a UK newspaper.

After apparently seeing his mother shot in the thigh, young Elliott Prior is said to have confronted the gunman shouting, "You're a bad man, let us leave."

Incredibly the gunman was moved to have pity on Elliott and his six-year-old sister Amelie, giving the pair a Mars bar each and allowing them and their mother to leave the chaotic shopping mall in the middle of the terror attack.

Elliott's 35-year-old mother Amber was reportedly able to grab two more children - including a wounded 12-year-old boy whose mother had been murdered – before exiting the shopping mall and taking the children to safety.

As the group turned to leave, the gunman allegedly called after them saying the jihadists only wanted to kill Kenyans and Americans, not Britons. He pleaded with Amber to convert to Islam and begged: "Please forgive me, we are not monsters."

Based on an article by DOYLE MURPHY in THE NEW YORK DAILY NEWS on Wednesday, September 25, 2013.

WRITING REFLECTION

Love And Destruction

Sometimes, I wake up saddened by the situation of the world. Different places come to my mind- Syria, Egypt, Sudan, The Philippines, and even on our home front of Chicago. We have forgotten that despite our many differences, we are one people. I feel that the cause of this estrangement is our tendency to stray from each other, as we drift away from the Love Source within ourselves.

Many of us live without a real intimate relationship with the Universal Love within us. Our violent and destructive history as a race has been a painful learning process of growing and evolving. One of the most important lessons, maybe the most important one, is to realize our union with the Infinite Consciousness that lives within our hearts. It has many names – the I Am, the Eternal Self, the Divine Soul, the One Mind, God, the Creator, etc. When we don't take time to cultivate an intimate relationship with that Source of Love within our being, life becomes confusing and frustrating.

Before we reach a place of emotional maturity, we tend to seek gratification from external sources in an effort to gain a sense of strength and connection. However, true inner strength cannot be found depending on external means. When we have such dependencies, we are operating from our defensive tendencies rather than from our Expanded Self. All the unnecessary strife and destruction originates from fear and defensiveness. On one hand, we want others to validate us, and on the other hand, we project our fears onto others and see them as the enemy, being dependent on others for our sense of self. We are, then, driven to be defensive. We get attached to "being right," having power over others, controlling life, people, and situations. We can drown in the hunger to keep that power going, keep feeding our defensiveness and justifying it. In this way, we create a cycle of destruction that will eventually take us down with it.

LOVE AND DESTRUCTION

We are designed to be sustained by our wholeness; a natural element of wholeness is the desire and the ability to connect. We thrive when we truly connect to ourselves and others. We yearn to share and know one another. Nothing makes us more joyful than giving and receiving love. The desire to connect is a powerful force. It can move us beyond our tendency to separate. We need to commit to loving connections on a daily basis, practicing this as a way of being. It is not an easy task, but what is more important than a loving, open heart, guided by wisdom?

WRITING REFLECTION

_____

_____

_____

Kidnapping: A Hole In The Soul

-The rescue of Hannah Anderson is the latest case of kidnapping that has sent ripples around the nation. It is raising concerns about children's safety. Luckily, this Californian teenager was rescued within days of that horrific incident, but not before being traumatized indelibly. This incident coupled with so many others that we have witnessed in the recent past, begs the questions- what drives perpetrators to commit these depraved crimes and, how do these holes develop in certain people's souls?

Whether we use substances, relationships, self-glamorizing means, or engaging in abuse of others to cover our suffering, we will fail. None of these compensations can ever really fill up the inner deficit of love for self or others within the soul. It is this deficit that creates our suffering.

On the "suffering menu," I see two kinds of suffering:

1. Natural, unavoidable suffering; and
2. Self-inflicted, self-maintained suffering.

Birth, aging, illness, and loss of loved ones are some of the natural and unavoidable causes of suffering. These are offered to us, along with the joy of birth, the wisdom of aging, the lessons of illness, and the love for others – a mixed bowl of sweet cherries and bitter almonds. Resisting any of these will not prevent us from being born, aging, falling sick, losing, or dying. Resistance only intensifies our experience of suffering. Still, we resist. Can you see the face of fear behind the resistance? Acceptance, spiritual and emotional openness, and communication are naturally the better choice. They can help to gently guide us through the necessary storms of loss and change.

The other kind of suffering, the self-inflicted one, is unnecessary, insidious, and deeply painful. When we keep daggering our own chests mechanically and relentlessly with destructive self-criticism, judgment, rejection, and shame – the torture, although hidden, is constant. When we exile our emotional selves to live on a small, lonely island, or in a cellar for the guilty and the unworthy, we slowly wither and grow bitter.

If we don't confront our suffering, we end up destroying ourselves and others. Our suffering should be our inspiration to become more loving people.

WRITING REFLECTION

_____

_____

_____

Lack Of Awareness: The Cost

The most precious gift we have as human beings is our ability to be aware. It gives us the power to witness our thoughts, feelings and actions and to meditate on them, learn lessons and evolve.

The earth, including the plant and animal kingdom, operates instinctively guided by the laws of nature. Man has the privilege of consciously guiding his / her actions, thoughts and feelings.

What are we doing with this gift?

The lack of awareness can cause problems for yourself and other people. This week, in Brooklyn, there was a young couple killed in a car accident by a person who lacked self-awareness. Man's lack of care for the natural world indirectly cost a Florida man his life when a sinkhole opened up beneath his home. New York City Mayor Michael Bloomberg created a campaign to fight teen pregnancy by making teens aware of the high cost of having a child.

Look at your life and consider the cost of a lack of awareness for yourself and others. This can bring a heightened sense of understanding. We all have some blind spots, areas of consciousness that are not fully developed. These are the ones we need to pay attention to most.

We are constantly evolving, being co-creators with the Source. We sculpt art; construct buildings, institute laws, etc. Since we are here to contribute to the quality of life, we need to evaluate our thoughts, feelings and actions on a daily basis.

Choose an area in your life that demands more awareness and ask yourself these three key questions.

1. How am I causing what is happening in this area of my life?
2. Why?
3. What do I need to shift within me to create positive expansion in this area?

WRITING REFLECTION

_____

_____

_____

Love And Shooting

This section was written in December of 2014 regarding the Shooting at Sandy Hook Elementary in Newtown, CT.

The contradiction between Christmas, the season of love and unity and the massacre of children in Newtown, Connecticut, is poignant and disturbing. Today, walking down the street, I watched the Christmas trees being sold, waiting to be placed in cheerful homes. They looked lonely and sad to me. Usually, their scent and beauty ignite within me a flicker of joy and expectation and a promise of love and unity. This year, this promise feels empty. On the way to Christmas mass, people are buying more guns.

Many of our youth are angry, lost, and emotionally empty because we are poisoning our environment and ourselves slowly but surely. Driven by materialism and commercialism, we seem to forget to invest in our souls. More importantly, we forget to invest in our youth. They are not being provided with emotional, spiritual and artistic guidance and inspiration. They are growing up in a society that respects status, money, and fame more than the Earth or basic human qualities without which there is no life. When and how are they supposed to receive the nurturing ingredients that will help them become loving and contributing members of society?

WRITING REFLECTION

_____

_____

_____

Hurricane Sandy: Gaining Knowledge From Tragedy

This section was written in November 2012 regarding the devastation Hurricane Sandy caused in New York City.

The haunting devastation to nature and people we have been witnessing over the last few days are heart-breaking for me and I'm sure for all of us. People lost all that is sacred and meaningful to them. Some have lost their homes and others have lost their loved ones. Unfortunately, there are those that have lost both.

How do we cope with this kind of tragedy?

How do we overcome these losses?

Yes, we try to stay positive, to help each other, and to find hope and rebuild. There are some things that cannot be replaced and the heart cries within. Some scars will remain for a long, long time.

Whenever I confront hardship, in my life, I always look deep within myself. It is important to me to understand what I can learn from any loss. Where and how do I contribute to the situation knowingly or not? What do I need to shift-see, be or do differently? How do I gain strength and wisdom from this situation? How do I use this as leverage or a jumping board to a higher state of being? This tragic storm has made me ask these questions.

I asked myself how did I contribute, how have we contributed to the weather changes that have been striking different parts of the world for the last few years? It feels as if Mother Nature is buckling under the constant abuse of toxins and violations we keep imposing on her. Did we cross the red line? Are we paying for it? This is a foreboding sign, and it is something we must acknowledge. Every one of us has the power to change and rebuild. We must rebuild for the better.

The way to rebuild is to take the lesson to heart and change the way we relate to nature. Taking the right actions in our daily lives and voicing our opinions, both socially and politically, will help us reclaim a sense of being part of the solution and not of the problem. Let us honor our lives, each other, and the Earth that takes care of us.

WRITING REFLECTION

_____

_____

_____

Living In A Disconnected World

We tend to seek a sense of gratification and validation from external sources in an effort to receive a sense of strength and connection. By so doing, we separate ourselves even further from our own essential identity, and as a result, further from our true inner power, love, and wisdom.

Let's take the example of a movie projector. The Source within is the light of the projector which makes the showing of our life's movie possible. We tend to identify strongly with the images and events that are projected onto the screen of our lives. If we become too attached to them, we can lose the connection with the light source that is actually the cause of all manifestations. Here is another example. Imagine that you're trying to wipe out a dirt mark on your face while looking in the mirror, and instead of wiping your face, you try to wipe the mark in the mirror, not realizing that you are the source of the real image. The people and the things that we become are so dependent on the containers of the exact light that is available to us. What we're looking for lives within us. We are what we are seeking. Fulfillment is already available within every cell of our being. All we need to do is experience a union with ourselves. The love we're looking for is conveniently located within our hearts. You can live the greatest love affair by celebrating the union between your human self and the Universal Self.

Since we don't always experience this union, we feel lonely and needy. We seek and depend on people and things outside of ourselves. We cultivate attachments, and we fear to lose them: we hold on, and we try to control and manipulate them in order to feel secure, thereby creating further isolation and suffering. We are designed to be sustained by our wholeness. One of the natural elements of wholeness is the desire and the ability to connect. Connecting is different

LET THE HEART SPEAK

from desperate dependency. We thrive when we truly connect with ourselves and others. We yearn to share and know one another. Nothing makes us more joyful than giving and receiving love from a place of openness and self-acceptance. The desire to connect is a powerful force. It can move us beyond our tendency to separate.

WRITING REFLECTION

_____

_____

_____

Mutual Responsibility

This section was written in 2012 in response to the Aurora shooting that killed 12 people and injured 70 others at a Century movie theater in Aurora, Colorado.

The tragedy that happened in Colorado is disturbing and sad, especially in lieu of the knowledge that it could've been averted. Part of being a community is taking notice of others, paying attention to their needs and emotions. James Holmes, the man accused of the shooting rampage, mailed a notebook, outlining his plans, to his psychiatrist days before the attack.

If this notebook was found and dealt with accordingly, it could have made a huge difference in peoples' lives. Tragedies happen when good men don't act. It might be naive to think James Holmes could have been stopped. Nevertheless, it is necessary to consider it.

It is a known fact that we are interdependent, much like the ecosystem. This is the nature of life; it is time to work with it rather than against it.

WRITING REFLECTION

_____

_____

_____

Inspiration In A World Of Bad News

We are saturated with bad news. From TV to radio, to the internet, such news seems to be the only focus point. We are being drawn into the baseline levels of humanity. When we give our attention to these distressing events, we are lending them our energy and we get depleted emotionally, physically, and spiritually.

Our bombardment with negative energy is stifling, impeding and inhibiting the intake of positive energy. The focus on the negative is counterproductive to transformation. Only a positive mind state encourages self-actualization. With that in mind, I want to share some stories with you to enlighten the heart and uplift the spirit:

CEO Of OMGPOP, Hired Back Laid-Off Workers

- Prior to Draw Something; the company of OMGPOP was in dire straits. In fact, the company had to lay off a good number of its workforce. When the popular app hit the stores and the $210 million Zynga offer came in, CEO Dan Porter hired back everyone that was laid off so they can all enjoy the benefits.

The Man Who Sold His Life On eBay After A Divorce, Finds Love, And Buys A Caribbean Island

- After his 2008 divorce, Ian Usher wanted a new life. So he did what any reasonable man would. He sold everything he had on eBay and went off, into the world, to check things off his bucket list. Now he's found a new love, is almost done with his list, and resides on an island. A perfect example of how letting go frees you up for better things.

INSPIRATION IN A WORLD OF BAD NEWS

Health Care Spending On Unnecessary Tests Discouraged By Major Medical Groups

- Are you tired of costly unnecessary testing? It seems like doctors are too. Organizations representing doctors have started the "Choosing Wisely" campaign. It's good to see that the bottom line is not necessarily the only line.

Girlfriend's Tweet Saves Carjacking Victim in South Africa

- A perfect example of how a "Tweet" can save a life. Moreover, it shows what can be done if we work together.

I hope these stories inspire, invigorate and open your eyes to the world that is all around us. If there is a time to focus on the positives, it is now. I make it a point to hear, read or learn about one positive story a day that would inspire my respect and admiration towards people doing good in our world.

WRITING REFLECTION

_____

_____

_____

The Inner Paradigm

This section was written in March of 2012 regarding the shooting of Trayvon Martin.

Creating a positive state of being is the most important step in the process of manifestation. Everything in the universe is actually energy (vibrations). The universe expresses itself by pulsating energetically. We are part of, and one, with this ocean of vibrations. We can change the frequency of our energetic combination by changing our feelings and thoughts.

We are endowed with free will and have the ability to shift our perspective. In this way, we co-create with the Universal Mind. This ability to master our energetic field is a gift deserving our responsibility and attention. It is important to become aware of it and what it creates within us and outside of us. If your state of being is disruptive to yourself and others, it is your responsibility to learn how to shift it.

The saddening and intertwined story of Trayvon Martin and George Zimmerman illustrates the way thoughts and feelings create reality. George Zimmerman was the captain of the neighborhood watch and had a pattern of calling the police without substantiated reason. This shows a state of agitation and perhaps a state of fear. Is it possible that his state of mind affected his violent action?

His violent reaction could have been prevented if he was in the habit of examining his inner reactions. If we live with unexamined inner violence, it seeks out targets, potential enemies, and volatile situations. We attract these circumstances to ourselves. Our reality is formed by our thoughts, feelings, and beliefs. When we live with judgment, anger, and fear we see the world through those glasses; it becomes our reality.

We all have a choice and there are always options: create the possibility of peace within yourself.

WRITING REFLECTION

JOURNEY TO BLISS

I Am Of The Earth

In one of the quiet nights when the world was deeply asleep, I was wide awake. A slow string of memories was moving through the sky of my mind like tear loaded clouds. Somehow, all the lonely, orphan like moments of my past, came in to say hello (or maybe to say goodbye?). Memories of times I felt bone-deep lonely and soul-filled sad. I was young then and did not realize yet, how loved, protected, and guided I truly was. I was sitting all chilled in the midst of enveloping warmth, hopeless while in the arms of bliss.

"You are of the Earth," I said to my soul, "like a tree, a fish, a bird, or a rock. How can you be a part of the earth and be orphaned? A piece of grass is always at home. A fish knows it is part of the ocean. It is time to know," I said to my soul. "It's time for the sadness to say goodbye to its old music and discover a new melody. Time to find the peaceful trust in the embracing warmth." "Yes," said my soul, "Let's do it!" "Ok," I said, "How about getting some sleep?"

WRITING REFLECTION

_____

_____

_____

Passion For Integrity: Lessons From My Cleaning Lady

My cleaning lady, Joslyn, is an amazing example of passion for integrity. She gets into all the seen and unseen crevasses of the house. Nothing escapes her scrutinizing eye. She stands for absolute cleanliness. Why am I writing about this? It is because I believe that no matter what you do, you can do it with a passion for excellence and a sense of integrity. Many of us don't. When how you do things matters to you, it means that you matter to you, others matter to you, and your projects matter.

I look at Joslyn when she works. She is totally in the moment. She's very present and most of the time, singing something or another in an untrained voice that is full of light-hearted peace. She is an example of mindfulness and respect for her work. I am sure she did not read any books about mindfulness or integrity. She did not attend any workshops. She is just fully engaged and takes pride in her job and the subtle healing magic of cleanliness.

A clean house breathes differently. A clean house lets you relax and be. It is a space for clarity and peace. To me, Joslyn's work is house therapy. If each of us did what we do with thorough dedication and love, the world would slowly heal and life would come to be what it wants to be: a flow of creative exchanges.

WRITING REFLECTION

_____

_____

_____

Beginners Guide To An Ease Of Being

I was watching my breath in one of my meditations, enjoying the soothing rhythm of taking in, holding, and letting go. When I don't get tight, by passing thoughts that interfere, if I stay present and surrender to the flow, I ride the wave. A feeling of ease and freedom washes over me.

So much of our life is wasted on resisting the natural flow. We live in "trying" to be this or that, "trying" to be good, perfect, beautiful, loved, clever, better, and best. We "try" to control our feelings, our reactions our expressions, other people, other things- endless efforts of "trying." All of the "trying" is a significant interference with the flow. What flow? The flow of our breath, our energy, our feelings, and our life force. Not a very smart thing to do, but being anxious and insecure, we are "trying" to make ourselves safe in this very unsafe, unhappy way.

It took me years to convince myself to give up the effort and enjoy the rhythm of life. The grand rhythm we see, feel, and live, when we let ourselves, moves through three phases. Creating, maintaining, and dissolving just like our breath does. Taking in, which is filling up with new breath; pausing to enjoy it and letting it go. Nature in its wisdom, creates anew, maintains, and then dissolves to create again and so on.

We're right now in the dissolved part of the cycle. All the leaves are dying, nature is letting go, to clear the plate for creating anew. I remind myself daily to live in a state of constant allowing. Allowing things and people to be what they are. Allowing myself to be; allowing life to be. This does not mean, not influencing transformation or creating beauty and goodness. It just means doing it from a place of ease of being. From a much more effective, organic, and authentic inner source. Find out what helps you to let go of the anxious and insecure effort so you can find your ease of being.

WRITING REFLECTION

_____
_____
_____

Free Your Energy Field

The whole universe is a grand symphony of energy. We are energy fields dancing, ideally free, and joyous within it. Otherwise and not so ideally, we would find ourselves somewhat stuck. All destructive, unworkable, and imbalanced patterns and their wide range of impacts are the results of energy that is trapped. This includes diseases of the mind, body, and soul; as well as social, political, and ecological imbalances. We are all witnessing these imbalances within our lives and everywhere around us. We need to remember that the universe continues to expand and is relentlessly keeping us within its flow of evolution. It is not supporting our hampering defensiveness, and it keeps pushing us beyond it.

Since balance and expansion start within each one of us, we need to learn to observe, moment to moment, how we handle our energy. Do we contract? Deny? Repress? Control? Are we allowing the flow of feelings and sensations to move through? We are responsible for freeing our energy and creating ourselves as the vibrant and expressive beings that we are meant to be.

Make it a point to notice when you get reactive, tight, defensive, or wilt away. In that moment, and actually in each and every moment to moment, make a choice to relax, open up, and allow emotions and sensations to flow and move. Open the door for them consciously by breathing, accepting, and letting what is be. Fear, pain, and anger are all forms of energy. When we allow them to move through our energy field, we expand and become more grounded in our spirit.

With all the emphasis on good Chi or good Feng Shui, it is also important to get into the habit of regularly checking the energy flow in your home and surroundings. One of the basic ways to check the energy flow in your home is to imagine Chi as water. If water were to flow into your home from the main door, where would it stagnate? Would it be free to harmoniously flow to all the areas of your space, gently refreshing them? Would it rush out of the back door, or would it get stuck in certain corners? Your inner energy, your environment, and the exchange of energy between yourself and others, are all opportunities for freedom and openness.

Your spirit wants to expand, your emotions to flow. It's up to you to keep the door open.

Now, let's discuss the physical elements of your life that are serving you just as your physical body does. These include:

- Home (spacing, comfort, inspiring energy)
- Personal Belongings (clothes, books, papers, personal objects)
- Large Objects (cars, tools, computer, television, instruments)
- Finances (bills, budget, designing the flow of money).

Take a look at this list. Make your list of things that you would like to enhance, give out, change, repair or acquire in order to create the physical, tangible structure of your life. These elements create a basic support structure. By attending to them, you are rewarding yourself with a sense of harmony.

WRITING REFLECTION

_____

_____

_____

How The Eagle Lost Its Beak

Change is essential to healing. The trials and tribulations to become "you" are an everyday process. Today, I would like to share with you a tale I found inspiring.

We all know of eagles. Their majestic features, their ferocity, and their hunting power show their strength of character. There is a Native tale that talks about how eagles live up to 70 years, but at the age of 40 are faced with a harsh decision.

In its 40th year, its long and flexible talons can no longer grab prey which serves as food. Its long and sharp beak becomes bent, its old-aged and heavy wings, due to their thick feathers, stick to its chest & make it difficult to fly. Then the eagle is left with only two options: DIE or go through a painful process of CHANGE which lasts 150 days. The process requires that the eagle fly to a mountain top and sit on its nest. There the eagle knocks its beak against a rock until it plucks it out. Then the eagle will wait for a new beak to grow back and then it will pluck out its talons.

When its new talons grow back, the eagle starts plucking its old-aged feathers. After 5 months, the eagle takes its famous flight of rebirth and lives for 30 more years.

To become a better person, the person you really wish to be, you must change. You must recognize the part of yourself that needs to dissolve, the part of yourself that is holding you down, keeping you a prisoner. Once you realize it, the process of letting go can start. You begin to shed parts of yourself and allow new parts to grow. Pain and struggle are part of our transformation, as are victory and liberation.

Like the eagle, we must tear off our worn pieces and begin anew.

Once those pieces have been removed, new ideas, habits, and experiences can take their place. Finally, from there we'll be able to fly anew.

WRITING REFLECTION

_____

_____

_____

Take A Vacation

I, like many of us, look forward to a vacation; a moment to pause, to rest, to empty the mind and open the heart to the simple delights of life. No matter how hard we try to balance our lives, most of us are constantly rushing to meet deadlines and complete projects. Gates of Power® Method emphasizes the importance of balancing quiet, internal, "me time," rest, play, emotional and physical care with life path, projects and goals. I am deeply committed to this balance in my life. In spite of my daily balancing act, I know when I need just to do nothing; to feel like a four-year-old with no to do lists, no responsibilities, nowhere to go, and nothing to do that is required. That letting go leads me naturally to a sense of joy and an appreciation for each moment.

When we stop, breathe and open up, we make new friends; we see things we didn't notice before, and we realize our love for people and the world all over again. We feel at one with life. Somehow, in this very troubled and divided world, our simple sense of safety has been robbed. A vacation can end tragically. In spite of such a possibility, we must not allow fears of the unknown dissuade us from exploring. Instead, let's learn to revisit that relaxed innocent space of a vacation, the adventure zone. Take yourself there. Give yourself that gift.

WRITING REFLECTION

_____

_____

_____

Have You Ever Wanted To Fly?

I was visiting my sister in Florida earlier this year. We stayed in a little hotel by the beach. Taking a long walk on the soft sand, barefoot under the smiling sun, is one of my favorite things to do. I know I'm not the only one. Walking on the beach brings with it an innocent feeling of being seven, free and one with the elements. What a sweet and refreshing feeling!

On one of my walks, I was observing a large group of seagulls having a crumbs party on the sand. As I came close, they scattered. Some flew to the sky, others dived into the water. At that moment, it dawned on me that the seagulls have the ability and the freedom to enjoy the three domains of nature: the sky, the water, and the land. They can move from one domain to the other with graceful ease. The whole of nature seems to be their playground. What a great way to live.

I had a moment of envy; I too wanted to be a seagull. Then, I realized that we humans have the same freedom within our souls. Physically, we can enjoy the Earth, the water, and the sky (skydiving, sky-gliding, etc.). But what's more important is that our souls can soar to the dimensions of visions and dreams unseen to the naked eye (sky), delve into the waters of emotions (water), and enjoy the earthly senses of life (land).

We are all soul seagulls. We just need to free ourselves from fears that bind us, preventing us from soaring as high as we can, or delving as deep as possible. Summer is a time of relaxation, it hands us our yearly invitation to shed some old fears, and provides a new sense of freedom to flower.

Accept the invitation and renew yourself.

WRITING REFLECTION

_____

_____

_____

The Power Of Choice

This section was written in June of 2015 in response to the Church Shooting in Charleston, South Carolina.

A week ago, Dylann Roof walked into a Sunday church mass at Emmanuel African Methodist Episcopal Church in Charleston, South Carolina. For an hour, he was a part of the congregation, joining in prayers and spirituals. Somewhere between the time of his entrance and departure, he shot and killed 9 of the 13 churchgoers in the congregation.

We all find ourselves at times, intensely enraged, upset, and even violent. In those moments, we have a choice. Either to react defensively or to go within, and sit with ourselves and acknowledge what is the cause of our suffering. None of us are immune to violent emotions; they are part of being human. It's what we do with them that make a difference.

Controlling your emotions does not resolve them. Emotions need to be acknowledged, accepted, understood, and then within our own self, or in a therapeutic setting, be moved, released, and expressed. In this way, they can get integrated, and become a source of strength and wisdom, rather than a source of suffering and inner irritation. Educationally and culturally, we don't really receive the tools to do that, which leaves our emotions bottled up to fester and eventually explode in a destructive way.

I believe that since we cannot avoid suffering, we should make the best of it. As far as I am concerned, there is nothing wrong with suffering. It seems to be an integral part of living: it tenderizes the soul and deepens our compassion; it inspires us to create, and, most importantly, it nudges us to transform.

LET THE HEART SPEAK

We need to respect our suffering as much as we respect our desire for happiness. Suffering, if we move through it with compassion and awareness, is a great mentor. It is, in fact, our guide to happiness. As we listen attentively to our suffering, we discover what our soul is crying for. Our longings and needs tell us what's most important to us. By listening closely, we can distinguish between addictive, compulsive cravings and true soul needs. Once we distinguish our needs, we can learn to nurture and guide them.

WRITING REFLECTION

_____

_____

_____

On Prayer

What comes to my mind are the ideas of spiritual teacher, Joel Goldsmith, who explains that we should understand ourselves as the instruments of God and any good we can provide for others is in proportion to our ability to receive through open mindedness. We cannot reach the experience of being one with the Spirit through our mind alone. Our emotions, our soul, and our energetic field all must be involved in that realization. When we catch a glimpse of the nature of God, the Absolute, we begin to know our oneness with Him. We realize that there is no one else other than Him. He is all there, and He is all there is.

Now we can begin to relax into that oneness and stop trying desperately to reach God as if He is the old man sitting on the cloud. Being receptive and responsive allows us to experience our unity with the One. If we're looking up to God, wanting God to do something, give us something, fix something, we are approaching from desperation, trying to influence God to do our will. The realization that we are one with Him leads us to know that our true needs are understood and our highest good is being taken care of. It is then that we relax and allow ourselves to receive, and to surrender to the divine design. A different way of understanding prayer is not begging and beseeching God but being in a state of silence in which we feel united with the Spirit, receptive to grace.

Aligning our will with the will of the Creator is, to me, the wisest and healthiest way to live. It leads to peace and to a greater ability to serve and contribute since it offers us the highest point of view and the ultimate support.

An excerpt from:

"**Gates of Power:** _Actualize Your True Self_" by Nomi Bachar

LET THE HEART SPEAK

WRITING REFLECTION

_____

_____

_____

Am I Going To Be Here The Next Moment?

It might be that I aged, slowed down, and sobered up, or it might be that I finally have clarity, that I have washed off all the mind, heart mud and can finally be present here in this experience called life. The bitter sweetness of it is penetrating, almost daggering, and softly embracing all at once.

I was sitting with a friend who is struggling with cancer. The struggle has stripped all his walls, masks, and hiding tunnels. He is alive now more than ever even while in a frail and withering body. Another friend struggling with cancer looked at me across the table with a soft and glowing smile lighting her face, a beautiful face that wrinkled overnight. She surrendered to the love and support of others, and learned to take in love; sickness takes us there.

Then, there are the shootings and the bombs. One moment someone you love is there, the next, they're gone. Each and every moment is beaming with preciousness, and I am feeling their pulse as if for the first time.

Life and death mixed inseparably – what is there to be, to do, to have? Just experience one moment after another. Stay open, touch, feel, see, and accept. We can keep creating from the heart, give and receive and just enjoy the gift of being alive. In one fleeting moment, it can all change.

WRITING REFLECTION

_____

_____

_____

Joy In The Journey

Adventures keep us young in spirit. They water the soil of the soul and fuel our aliveness. They keep our brain functioning better and our hearts excited. What constitutes adventure is unique for each person. Some of us might want to climb the Himalayas, skydive, or take a long sailboat journey. For others, it can be new museums, a night at the opera, a different jazz class, a new course, or the zoo, if we have not been there for a while. An adventure is anything new—or old— that feels new and exciting. Every day should have a little adventure in it. A new dish for dinner, a possible new friend, a new or different route to get home, a new book, a new idea, a new plan. Keep generating adventures for yourself. I recommend keeping a running list of adventures experienced and desired. Remember, adventures don't have to consist of a trip to China; they could be as simple as a new song on your playlist.

WRITING REFLECTION

_____

_____

_____

Tips On Growing Your Blissipline

Blissipline is a spiritual practice. It's the path to creating, maintaining, discovering, and living in the inner place of bliss which resides within your Expanded Self. We all yearn to tap into the flow of natural joy, love, and playfulness and learn to express it. If you can think of moments in your childhood when you were a little bliss bubble, walking around, giggling, crying, laughing, and playing - full of curiosity and awe - you are clearly remembering the YOU that is still there.

Our life experiences often go partially unexamined, unresolved, and unreleased. The easiest and most common way is to create a negative assumption about our difficult experiences instead of acknowledging, releasing, and integrating them to create a sense of strength. Imagine your joy bubble, that true child-like self of yours, encrusted in layers of self-made mud.

There's no need to blame ourselves for our mud creation. There is a need to realize that it is only mud and that we can begin to take some of it off to spiritually, emotionally and psychologically shower ourselves. It helps to let go slowly and continuously of what we are not (constricting thoughts, feelings, limiting beliefs, and stories) and connect to our blissful self - the unconditional loving joy of the universe residing within our heart. Blissipline is unveiling more of who we truly are, and inevitably, it involves a level of love, acceptance, and intimacy with ourselves.

Our Defensive Self resists this process and is threatened by it. It pulls us away from our joy with busyness, drama, distractions, addictions, and projections. This is understandable. Furthermore, we may not be conscious that we're acting out of our Defensive Self. The first step is realizing our avoidance of ourselves, of our deeper feelings, and thus our avoidance of experiencing the moment and life around us.

LET THE HEART SPEAK

This is the first and the most continuous step since this avoidance of truth and the moment can be very insidious, subtle, and deceptive. One can master the spiritual intelligence to identify it and let it go, moment-to-moment, allowing the truth to blossom.

WRITING REFLECTION

_____

_____

_____

A Fight For Freedom

A sense of freedom has always been one of my most passionate pursuits. As a young adult, I wrapped myself in the bondage of fears, insecurities, and doubts. My lifelong journey has been colored by my deep desire to find inner freedom as well as the freedom to express, create, and contribute. My journey took many curves, and it still continues to flower.

It pains me to hear that there are frequent on-going battles of freedom occurring all around the world. Within the past two years, millions of people in areas such as the Middle East and Africa have died attempting to escape the oppression in their homeland, gain a sense of dignity and a chance at a free life. Watching the migrants struggle for basic freedom made me think of my struggle to survive as a Jew and an Israeli. Having this struggle moves me to identify with all people fighting for their basic right to live dignified and expressive lives. This is not something I take for granted. I leave you with some thoughts expressed by the Dalai Lama.

He once spoke about how the Universal Declaration of Human Rights was established in 1948 to ensure the all-inclusive right of freedom to all people. Essentially, he says that a violation of human rights anywhere restricts the fullness of human rights everyone; as we are one people. The denial of the fact that human rights are being infringed upon in certain places, is to deny the truth. He urges that peace cannot be had if we do not fight for the whole of humanity instead of acting in our own interest.

Let's remember that life and humanity is sacred. Cultivate your life for yourself and others, since, in reality, you are others and they are you in reality.

LET THE HEART SPEAK

WRITING REFLECTION

_____

_____

_____

Death In The Middle Of Life

My heart knew when the phone rang at 6:30 in the morning on Saturday. My brother's shaky voice on the other line confirmed my feelings, my mother had passed away. He said he held her hand as she released her young and buoyant spirit through the open gate. Life stood still at that moment. My room was holding its breath. It felt like the ticking of my clock, the New York City sirens, and the blowing wind had paused, and paused. My best friend left and I did not get to say goodbye. I didn't ask for a phone number either, or look for some way to reach her in those other worlds, the way I usually did daily on the phone.

How does one go on without that one person who always and forever loved you more than you could ever love yourself?

Then, there was the mad rush to the plane and the 12 long hours to get to Israel, grasping while reflecting on the details of life through frozen tears and a crushed heart. I held my brother and sister tight when I stood before her small, 97-year-old earthly cage at the funeral. I looked at the many faces that came to say goodbye and saw a large circle of love. The words that finally sprang out of my mouth came from a deep well of gratitude:

"Mom, you taught us to cling to life. To live it fully and passionately. To stand up for what we feel is right. To dream big and go for it. To find joy and love everywhere we go, and let them nurture us. Most importantly, to trust the loving and guiding hand of God and the innate goodness of his universe. Thank you for the bright light you left within our souls, and the path you illuminated just by being yourself."

LET THE HEART SPEAK

WRITING REFLECTION

_____

_____

_____

The Seeds Of Your Soul

All of your goals and dreams are seeds of fulfillment lying dormant in the soil of your soul just like seeds in the winter earth that await spring to fully blossom. The same power of manifestation and growth lives within you. Nature has given you the power to realize your dreams and potential, but it is your personal responsibility to nurture them and bring the seeds of your desire to life.

I am sure that you have asked yourself, "Why are some people successful in achieving their goals and others are not?" Now, ask yourself," why am I able to manifest certain goals in my life and not others?"

Here are some possible reasons:

1. **Low self-esteem**
2. **Old limiting internal imprints (unresolved trauma, suppressed emotions)**
3. **Not taking full responsibility for one's life**
4. **Fear of commitment**
5. **Fear of failure and success**
6. **Inefficient work habits (procrastination, lack of organization)**
7. **Lack of clarity and focus.**

Take a look at the list and circle one or few of the reasons that might be inhibiting your progress, if you are serious about achieving your goals and dreams, you must embrace change and empower yourself to dissolve the inner blockages that stop you. Do not judge yourself for it as we all have to overcome internal challenges. Your intentions, choices, and commitments create your reality. Feelings, beliefs and attitudes that limit you need to shift. Effective counseling can help you move through repressed imprints and restricting beliefs to create a space of openness and greater expansion.

Let's look at the list again. All six of the above items stem from one specific one. **Can you guess which one it is?**

Let's say that you marked a lack of clarity and focus, fear of commitment, and low self-esteem. Ask yourself, "Which one is the cause and which ones are the symptoms?" In this example, the cause is the low self-esteem; the other two are symptoms of the cause.

Let's take another example. Say you chose fear of failure or success, lack of clarity or focus, and inefficient work habits. Ask yourself, "Which one is the cause, and which ones are symptoms?" In this case, your fear is the cause of the lack of clarity and the inefficient work habits. If we go deeper, we might realize that the fear is there because of poor self-image. So actually, the primary cause of our inability to manifest what we want might be the negative perception we have of ourselves and of our place in the world.

One of the most important seeds to attend to is the seed of our sense of self. It is also one of hardest ones to heal if wounded. What can help us is to realize that we are carrying within us the same consciousness, strength, love, and creativity that are found within the universal source. If we think that we are lacking, we need to remember that we are children of the Light. The Light lives within us as our true essence.

1. Our true essence is love

2. Our real power is our oneness with all things- the power of existence.

3. What we experience as a lack is an illusionary perception that can be dissolved.

This is the seed to cultivate from which your flower, unique and potent, will bloom.

WRITING REFLECTION

_____
_____
_____

The Biology Of Feeling

Everything exists within a unified field of consciousness and energy. Feelings are a whole body experience. Every cell feels, and every feeling is registered in each cell.

When we have a thought or feeling, the brain releases some chemicals known as neuropeptides- "neuro" because they were first found in the brain, "peptides" because they are protein-like molecules. Brain cells speak to one another through these chemical messengers. They "send" and "receive" communications, much like we dialogue with one another. When a cell wants to speak to another cell, it sends a neuropeptide that is received by the other cell's receptor, and communication is achieved. This communication was initially believed to be unique to brain cells. Through time, it was discovered that other cells generated the same chemical messengers and that these "receptors" existed in cells throughout the body.

As it turns out, our whole body is constantly thinking, feeling, and talking to itself. Every event within us is communal. When we say, "I have a gut feeling," we are not speaking metaphorically; our gut makes the same chemicals that our brain makes when it thinks. Our gut is talking to us. It is communicating its messages to the whole body, and we know how accurate "gut" feelings are.

Another example is our immune system. Its cells have receptors that can bind with chemical messengers when we are joyful, anxious, or peaceful; our immune cells are receiving the messages and are thinking and feeling with us. They are also producing messenger chemicals to communicate to our whole body and state of mind. In this way, immune cells are moving around in the body acting as a circulating nervous system. They are listening to every move within and without, ready to send, receive and respond immediately. Immune cells are like a mother who is tuned-in to her young child; she knows its need even before it does.

This symphony of communication is totally orchestrated and all systems work together in absolute coordination.

WRITING REFLECTION

_____

_____

_____

The Man On 23rd Street

My office is located on the 24th Street and 9th Avenue. Most people who walk on the 23rd Street between 7th Avenue and 9th Avenue have noticed an older, homeless man with kind features and long white hair. This homeless man has all his possessions piled into six or seven shopping carts. The carts are little mountains of all kinds of objects: Pillows, blankets, parts of furniture, newsletters, clothing, etc. Everywhere he goes, he needs to move his little train of carts with him.

At times, I see him having to move all the carts through a green light. Quite a difficult task indeed. At other times, he has to spread all of the carts along the Avenue so he can manage to get to where he's going. Looking at him, I wondered about the inner baggage that we all carry. Unresolved past experiences, unreleased resentments, judgments, collected concepts, beliefs, ideas that we embrace and internalize without discerning whether they truly belong to us or not. All of that weighs us down and renders us unavailable to truly be where we see things with fresh and unburdened heart and eyes.

Let's clear our inner house on a daily basis and allow our emotions to move through and release themselves. Letting go again and again of whatever constricts, burdens, and limits us. Let's remove objects that we don't need, people and relationships that are not nurturing to us any longer, and concepts that are blocking of us from living with an open heart.

WRITING REFLECTION

_____

_____

_____

How To Transform Pain Into Compassion

While we go through the heart of the winter with the long, dark, cold nights, it is good to remind ourselves not to resist the feelings that this season brings up in us. If we can keep ourselves open to these emotions and embrace them, we can move through them and open up space for the inner spring. Osho, one of my favorite teachers and writers, recommends a breathing technique that transforms pain into compassion.

He instructs to breathe in and imagine that you are breathing in all the darkness and negativity in your life. Welcome it into your heart. Stop trying to resist it, avoid it or destroy it. That has been taking up all of your energy. As you are breathing in this heaviness, let it be absorbed into your heart before you exhale. And then the moment you breathe out, breathe out a golden light. Breathe out your greatest lightness, your highest joy, love, and blessing from your heart into the source of the negativity. You can transform the darkness in your life with your breath.

When breathing out, express all the love that you have, the blissfulness, and the benediction. Pour your love onto existence. This is the method of compassion: drink in all the suffering and pour out all the blessings. And you will be surprised what happens when you really do it. The moment you stop resisting all the darkness and heaviness in your inner world, they are no longer sufferings.

He speaks about the power of the heart to transform any energy to light. The heart is a transforming force, the essential alchemist. It can drink in any misery, pain or sadness and transform it into lightness. He encourages trusting the power of the heart. Once you have learned

LET THE HEART SPEAK

that your heart can do this magic, keep practicing it again and again. You can transform the planet with the power of compassion.

WRITING REFLECTION

_____
_____
_____

Life Under The Snow

In the darkness and heaviness of winter, we sometimes feel that the cold will never lift. Similar to how we feel when we are stuck with sadness and despair gripping our hearts. If we can remember who we truly are, and what we have to give, we can slowly move from the heavy darkness into the light. Here is a poem that I wrote in one of those dark moments:

> There in the silence
> of dark snow covering my heart,
> I was holding my breath.
> My eyes wide open,
> my soul frozen,
> and the moments growing longer...
>
> I was listening,
> buried alive,
> frozen, Waiting
> to feel my pulse again,
> to see a ray of light,
> to know hope,
> to resurrect, and
> touch the corner of joy.
>
> So I can remember, I always am, always alive.

WRITING REFLECTION

_____

_____

_____

About Kabbalah: The Path Of Receptivity

Kabbalah, the Jewish mystical teachings, is more about losing ourselves, than about finding. Losing ourselves in the other, in the moment, in life, as opposed to being ego-centered. The literal translation of the word Kabbalah is, "that which is received." To be able to receive, we must become receptive, open ourselves, creating a vessel with which we can absorb that which we wish to understand, become, and express. Kabbalah, the path of receptivity, is about opening the soul to a higher reality, seeing the spirit within, and raising our consciousness to a point where our perception of reality is completely changed. Then the divine within all creation is revealed.

What is blocking our way from receiving and experiencing the truth of being is our Defensive Self, sometimes called the Ego. Our Defensive Self is grounded in fear, ignorance, and a consistent concern about survival. It is the fountainhead from which all negativity stems: vanity, stubbornness, anger, a need to control, etc. All spiritual paths teach us to become unidentified from this false sense of self. As we begin to observe our Defensive Self, we learn to guide and soften it, allowing our transcendent soul, or our Expanded Self, to shine through and be the navigator of our lives.

Kabbalah teaches, like all spiritual paths, that all that exist is Ein Sof (That which is without end.) As we clear our thoughts, feelings, and energy, we allow this experience of the Ein Sof to permeate our being, fading out the illusion of separateness, the experience of fear, and the strength of our Defensive Self. Slowly, the negative emotions which are our defensive reactions fade away.

In the season of gratitude, we need our openness and receptivity to feel the bounty and blessings in our lives and all around us. A much-needed practice in our life that is a lot focused on doing, accomplishing, and achieving.

Personally, I see receiving as my most important life lesson. Every morning, I dedicate being open and receptive to life and living. By noon, I have to remind myself again…

WRITING REFLECTION

_____

_____

_____

Thinking Is Not Living

This morning in my Yoga class, I found myself drifting away from the world of my sensations, to the world of my thoughts. The world of sensations and emotions is rich, vibrant, and colorful, while the world of thoughts can be flat and two-dimensional.

"Why am I here?" I asked myself every time I caught myself in the world of thoughts. Then I would tap myself on the shoulder, so to speak, like my old Zen master used to do to us, and say "Back to the moment you go."

In this morning's Yoga class, I had to guide myself back to the experience of being, over and over and over again. The habit of hiding away from life, in the cocoon of our thoughts is strong. Somewhere in the past, a threat, a painful or scary experience, had caused us to contract. We shrunk away from our life force, and from our moment to moment expansion. Then we became trapped in our safe smallness, and allowed our mind to entertain thoughts about life, instead of living it. In the thinking world, our breath is shallow, our energy moves slowly and sluggishly, our emotions are not fully experienced or expressed, and our thinking mind gets fatter and fatter. So now what?

First, one must ask oneself, "Do I want to live here, in this thinking world, or do I want to return to the living world?" Many choose to stay; some choose to return. If you choose to come back to living, get ready to muster a fierce commitment to regain your aliveness. It is a moment to moment choice to feel, to allow the energy to move, to accept what is there, to surrender, and let yourself slowly expand through the ups and downs of emotions, energy, and sensations. Slowly and surely, you become comfortable with living, and the river that is your being begins to merge into the universal grand flow.

WRITING REFLECTION

Opening Our Emotional Center

The heart, home to our emotions, is innocent and honest. When it is open, it is a source of love and joy, a generator of playful bliss and creative impulses. When the heart is closed, caged or repressed, our life force is blocked. We are not breathing, emotionally speaking, and we are not fully alive; we simply remain in a state of basic existence. The heart is also the master of our physical reality; it conducts the music which is the energy of our being. All physical manifestations are realized with the assistance of our feelings. If we are committed to being emotionally alive and physically healthy, we must return the heart to its open and magical nature.

All of our feelings are necessary, including the ones that are difficult and painful. Feelings help us survive, express ourselves, and transform. Each feeling contributes to our gaining self-knowledge, and to understanding others and life. For example, sadness can inform us about unfulfilled needs and longings, and it can move us to find ways to express them. Anger might inform us about our boundaries and bring to our attention any possible violation of them. Fear can alarm us or teach us to find courage, etc. The poetic, ecstatic and inspiring moments of our lives are born out of our ability to feel.

Since all feelings and emotions spring from the same source, the fact is that when you shut down the difficult ones like pain, fear or anger, you will shut down the blissful ones as well. There is no way around this fact. Cheating will not help. Each one of us needs to choose what we will commit to- an open or closed heart. Feelings and emotions are energies. Energy is indestructible. It does not die: it only changes form. We can bury our emotions, repress or deny them, but we can never kill them. They will keep hunting us and will manifest in our body, in our behavior and our everyday life. The good news is that since energy transforms, we can shift the energy of feelings from negative to positive. Here are tips on how to open up your emotional center.

1. Take time daily to get in touch with your feelings. Journaling is one great way to do that.

2. Teach yourself to accept and understand your emotions rather than to judge, criticize, or dismiss them.

3. Find a creative way to share and express your emotions.

4. Your emotions are your inner garden. Take responsibility for them. Transform the negative ones and cultivate the positive ones.

5. In emotionally difficult times, allow yourself to feel. At the same time, support yourself to find what makes you happy.

When you find emotional freedom, integration, and expression, you will be able to interact with life fully, as well as to give and receive love.

WRITING REFLECTION

_____

_____

_____

Why Are We Here?

This question becomes very urgent and relevant in the face of all that is happening in the world. It appears we **must** realign and unite as a human family to prevent destroying ourselves.

If you really connect with your soul, you find that you want to love, to share, and contribute. This is our highest nature. It looks like a lot of us have lost the connection to this very deep and basic yearning. Instead, we have an inner disconnection and emptiness for which we compensate by following the false gods of status, money, control and domination. In so doing, we leave a blazing trail of destruction, both behind us and ahead. We are here to follow our bliss, to realize and express the loving, creative, joyful nature of the Self.

I have been asked by many clients, "How do I find my personal purpose?" In other words, "How do I define my life's path?" My answer is always, "Ask this question as many times as needed in your meditations and listen to the answers." Answers can come through a feeling, an image, a word, or a combination of all these things. Some of us have a very clear sense of our Life Path. My brother, for example, is a brilliant mechanical engineer, started taking things apart and putting them back together when he was four or five. He loved nothing more than finding out how things work. To this day, this is what fascinates him.

On the other hand, I was led to pursue acting by a strange impulse that came over me when I was looking at an advertisement for the Academy of the Performing Arts. I remember being glued to the words, the dance, and acrobatics that appeared on the list of subjects being offered. I had no dance background, and I was one of the worst students in my high school gym classes. I also showed no acting talent whatsoever. I cannot explain my attraction to the advert other than to say that my soul was calling out. It knew that this was the path to follow.

If you have defined your talents, gifts, and pleasures, and you clearly enjoy engaging in certain activities and projects, it means, simple and clear, that you are supposed to do so. The famous quote by Joseph Campbell, "Follow your bliss," is not some new age fluff. It is a guiding principle for living a purposeful life. You are here to fulfill your potential and to contribute. These two are your rights and your responsibilities. Your talents, abilities, and passions live within you like the seeds of an apple tree, waiting to become fruits. It is wise to support and nurture them. Doing so, you are giving to yourself and others.

Many of us lack the courage to follow our bliss. We were taught that we should have a good job that pays the bills and that fulfillment is secondary. Not true. Fulfillment is primary. Ideally, we should find a creative way to marry our fulfillment with a good job that pays the bills.

A strong and consistent commitment to contributing to ourselves and others leads us to live a purposefully fulfilled life. Why else are we here?

WRITING REFLECTION

_____

_____

_____

Being A Powerful Communicator

To succeed in any area of life, to reach your potential and find fulfillment, you must become a good communicator. Take it upon yourself to cultivate the connector/communicator within you. Your Expanded Self is a wise and a compassionate communicator. Let it guide you in all of your relationships. Keep the following tips in mind as you seek to improve your communications:

- **Be the cause.** Stay present, which means committing to creating mutual understanding, mutual benefit, and mutual enjoyment, and taking responsibility for the success of the communication.
- **Keep an open mind and heart.** Be flexible, ready to learn, and ready to see things in a new way.
- **Focus on the other person.** Focus on the other person and see their value.
- **Find common ground.** Learn to see things from the other's perspective (even if, or when, you have a different opinion).
- **Be authentic and clear.** Use all five channels—thoughts, emotions, words, physical expression, and action.
- **Be a contribution.** Find how you can help, support, inspire, create change and express affection.
- **Use humor.** Playful enjoyment can contribute to almost all communications.

WRITING REFLECTION

_____

_____

_____

Generate Your Joy

How much time do you spend just playing? "Playing is for kids," we think. "I hardly have time to wash and set my hair or do my nails," said one of my clients, a full-time businesswoman with two kids. "You must be joking. I don't even have time to eat calmly or read for pleasure." I totally identify with her. I live in New York City, where the pace of life runs at least at double speed. Most active and working adults work from nine in the morning to seven or sometimes eight o'clock in the evening, with not much of a lunch break. Late dinners are often accompanied by the residue of take-home work. The household chores and attention to the kids usually takes up the little time that is left. Who can even think of playtime?

I have personally found that if I don't strongly commit to playtime and schedule it, I never get to play. Playtime has an amazing effect on my spirit. It is a great remedy for stress.

What is it that I mean by playtime? It means doing something that is purely pleasurable or silly and light-hearted, just for the sake of having a good time. This means different things to different people. For some, it's sitting around with friends, joking, laughing, and generating silliness. Others love the quiet of a chess game, puzzles, or board games. Others love to walk in nature or just sit under a tree or on the beach, watching the clouds and listening to the birds. There are also people who love to expend a lot of energy during their playtime activities. This might be a vigorous game of football, mountain climbing, rock climbing, or scuba diving. I suggest you make a list of your pleasures and do your best to schedule playtime with yourself and your loved ones. Daily mini playtimes and longer ones on the weekends are as necessary as food. Ultimately, you are here to experience joy and follow your bliss. Playtime is a fun step on the road to enlightenment.

WRITING REFLECTION

Freeing The Emotional Self

All the stages of our evolution are living within our Emotional Self: the baby, the child, the adolescent, and the adult. Nurturing parental love is necessary throughout our emotional development, especially in the early stages. When any one of these stages is disrupted, our needs are not met, our feelings become fragmented. As a result, our natural development is compromised, and the smooth transition from stage to stage is interrupted. It makes sense that it is beneficial to access the earliest stage that was disrupted.

By re-experiencing the emotional reality of it, including unmet needs, pain, and fear, we release repressed emotions and give ourselves the nurturance needed to heal and complete that stage successfully. At a young age, when our needs are not met, we get angry. This anger is a natural reaction. It is a cry for help and a protest against being ignored. Most of us were trained to repress pain and anger. When these feelings are repressed, excess neurotransmitters and other neuro-chemicals flood the brain and the whole system. Our receptors get clogged. As a result, a state of toxicity develops, which is a source of future emotional and physical disease.

The excess neurotransmitters overexcite the nervous system, causing symptoms that range from mild anxiety to mania or violent feelings. These symptoms are healing events, and it's best if they are not suppressed. If handled properly, these symptoms will not escalate to actual violence. When pain and anger are trying to surface and release, it is important to redirect these emotions toward our memories of the original abusers or wrongdoers. I stress this should be done as part of a therapeutic process and not any other way. Only when the anger and pain are expressed within a therapeutic process toward whoever feels like the source, can these feelings be released effectively.

At times, it takes some soul-searching and peeling off layers of hurt to truly discover why we are angry. Misdirected anger is very common. It can get triggered by our spouse, a neighbor, or the news. Instead of looking for the origin of our anger, we explode or attack the person or event that triggered it. These explosions can be called vicarious detoxification crises. Misdirected explosions don't remove repressed emotions; they only serve to continue the cycle of toxicity and our inner suffering.

Working with anger

We need to train ourselves to recognize the origins of our anger. When we realize that we are overreacting, we need to stop and look within, identify our emotions, and in a private, expressive, and creative way, address the source of our disgruntled feelings. It takes discipline to refrain from reacting to the present moment's trigger. Whatever triggered it only serves as a reminder of an unresolved relationship or event in the past.

The process of addressing the original source is a private event. It is your inner work. For example, I am not suggesting that you rage against your parent in person, even if they are the original abuser. Your emotions are directed towards the parent in your memories. In the process of redirecting your angry emotions, you are allowing yourself to become the child that could not express themselves, and you are encouraging the very expression of feelings and needs that are still held within you and waiting to be released and acknowledge. This process achieves two important goals: one—you get in touch with an important part of yourself that was repressed giving yourself the opportunity to heal and integrate it; two—you detoxify your body from the excess overload created by repressed emotions. Over time, this process dissipates the overload from the past and will ground us in the present moment. We are digging up the buried heart and teaching ourselves to feel. The process can be painful, but the loving guidance and awareness of our Expanded-Self help us re-integrate ourselves.

WRITING REFLECTION

_____

_____

_____

Suffering: The Hidden Gift

Aside from devoted masochists, who wants to suffer? We don't wait in line, eager to purchase extra suffering; most of us try to avoid it, chasing the lighter colors of life. But if we possess a serious passion for living, we need to look at the inspiring- yes, inspiring! - experience of suffering.

As an Israeli and a Jew, I should be very comfortable with the subject- yes, I am. Fortunately (or unfortunately), I come from a long tradition of suffering. Jews have mastered the skill of turning suffering into a spiritual goldmine.

We need to respect our suffering as much as we respect our desire for happiness. Suffering, if we move through it with compassion and awareness, is a great mentor. It is, in fact, our guide to happiness. As we listen attentively to our suffering, we discover what our soul is crying out for. Our longings and needs tell us what's most important to us. By listening closely, we can distinguish between addictive, compulsive cravings and true soul needs. Once we distinguish our needs, we can learn to nurture and guide them.

The power to transcend suffering and turn it into a blessing comes from the willingness to consciously experience, explore, and express our feelings. The treasures we find are invaluable truths about ourselves, others, and life, and a connection to our inner power. Suffering becomes destructive when we resist and deny ourselves the emotional experience, robbing ourselves of the precious opportunity to discover our truths and our power. Resisting, we get caught in the net of suffering; there, we either give up or, thrashing about, we get entangled, and eventually, destroy ourselves and others.

WRITING REFLECTION

An Invitation To Be

I invite you on a journey to full aliveness. "Full aliveness," is not a real expression per se, so you won't find it in a dictionary. Rather, it is my shorthand way to express the idea of being fully alive. If you are already on the path to full aliveness, enjoy the information and any new ideas or tools presented to you.

To me, full aliveness means self-expression, creativity, the capacity to feel all of our feelings, openness to love, adventure, and learning. It is the passion to actualize our vision and our deepest desires to create a life of contribution. I know it seems like a lot, but why not go as far as we can? Nature intended us to be the healthiest, best version of ourselves, and our dreams come true. Commitment, passion, and discipline are necessary companions on the journey. My book is here to assist you in the process. It is based on the Gates of Power® Method, a path to self–transformation and self-actualization.

On the one hand, it is important to be able to experience and accept all the aspects of living as a human being and on the other hand, to realize that we are beings of consciousness moving through a human life. Our journey is one of embracing our earthly existence, creatively and expressively, while at the same time coming to know our true nature as spirits, pure awareness, and ultimately one with the Absolute.

I have learned that what gives us the most fulfillment and happiness is the ability to be who we are and grow into our true power. Being who we are, as simple as it sounds, is not that easy. It takes time, awareness, self-knowledge, and courage. It is a life-long process of learning to accept and express ourselves, to give to and of ourselves freely, and confidently open up to receive and create happiness. We have a deep yearning to feel and know everything that lives within us. Since we're made of the same intelligence and energy that the whole universe is made of, we have a natural appetite to experience infinite possibilities within ourselves— an appetite that entices us to constantly grow, change and learn. This wonderful yearning for life is our jewel.

How is it then that sometimes it seems as though we are living alongside life, not really in it as if there is a glass wall between life and us? A sense of emptiness and sadness is born out of that. I remember myself in my twenties, sitting on a bus and watching a group of people my age laughing, kidding around, and being silly. It sounded like they were miles away. There was that glass wall feeling. I was so withdrawn and joyless at that point in my life that laughter and silliness were things I observed, not things I experienced.

I think of children before they lose their spontaneity, sense of curiosity, adventure, a presence of being, playfulness, creativity, and open-heartedness. They have the ability to love. They are empowered and moved by things around them. They *are* fully alive. We were all children at one time, then something happened to us, and we lost touch with our innocence, simplicity, and spontaneity. As adults, we do have extra responsibilities; we all have to grow up, but the loss of our openness and spontaneity is not a necessary part of growing up. Our personal life history, as well as the cultural and societal influences, can inhibit our capacity for being fully alive and present. In varying degrees, we lose touch with our spontaneity. At times, it is buried so deep that it feels like we cannot reach it.

Encourage yourself to make a commitment to find a path that takes you back to an open and expressive state of being. These abilities have not disappeared—we have just lost touch with some of them. We can reclaim them when we return to our source.

A beautiful poem by the Persian poet, Rumi about the journey back to ourselves struck me as I wrote this. I am not reproducing the entire poem here, but it is called "If A Tree Could Wander." It is widely anthologized and available on the Internet if you would like to look it up.

> *The drop that left its homeland,*
> *the sea, and then returned?*
> *It found an oyster waiting*
> *and grew into a pearl.*

When we become committed to our fulfillment, we begin to ask ourselves what really makes us happy. What brings us joy? What fulfills us? We're all unique, and our needs are different. Identifying our true wants and needs and honoring them is the first step to fulfillment.

WRITING REFLECTION

_____

_____

_____

Resolution: Restoring Flow

My personal New Year's Resolution is to further my ability to live by the four magic R's: **Relax, Release, Receive, and Rejoice**.

Since life is consciousness manifesting through energy, it make sense that the art of living consists of allowing our consciousness and energy to converge with that of the Source. Just like all rivers desire to merge with the ocean, our personal river of consciousness/energy yearns to flow freely and unite with the ocean of cosmic energy. Shouldn't we relax and enjoy this journey? Easier said than done. Our fears, doubts, defensive patterns and unresolved emotional hurts block the flow of energy-what are we to do?

The magic is in the choice. In each moment to moment, you should choose to allow emotions/sensations to move freely. Acknowledge what you feel and sense. Embrace it as good since it is energy, and let it be. Let it breathe. Let's remember that even fear, pain, and anger, the three emotions that we tend to shut down most, are just energy. When we let feelings and sensations be, they naturally restore themselves to become vibrations. They move along creating a healthy energetic flow.

The same is true for thoughts, concepts, and beliefs. If we can observe them and let them flow, which means not getting attached to them, or hide behind them, they become like clouds in the sky. They move, they shift, and they dissolve. We are truly the witness of the clouds, a place of pure awareness, and the blue sky. Imagine how it would feel not to be identified and righteous about your beliefs and thoughts. Just considering it makes me smile. What about you? Dwelling in a place of pure awareness lifts the burden of our compulsive thoughts and beliefs, and opens up in us a space for exploration, freedom, play, and simple enjoyment.

LET THE HEART SPEAK

A new year of letting go and letting flow is a good year.

WRITING REFLECTION

_____

_____

_____

How Is Your Blissipline Doing?

When we pay close attention to ourselves, we find out that our Defensive Self is constantly interfering with our natural flow of joy. It is relentlessly judging ourselves and others, criticizing, and trying to control everything around us. Deeply anxious and tremendously manipulative, our Defensive Self is making sure that we are SAFE at any cost and that cost includes our health and our happiness. Observing our Defensive Self and its continual acrobatics can be funny if we can separate ourselves from it and stand on the side with humor; but at the same time, it can be frustrating and tiring. As one of my clients said, "I feel I'm constantly kidnapped by my Defensive Self, and pushed into the realms of anxiety and reactiveness and I can't stand it." Our Defensive Self robs us of our peace of mind and the simple, natural, child-like joy within us that is waiting to be expressed.

I found myself laughing out loud when I heard my Defensive Self screaming at my blender. I was blending my morning shake while in a rush to get to a meeting when all of the sudden my blender started moving in a strange pattern. My Defensive Self kicked in and I heard myself yell at the blender, *"What?! What's wrong with you?!"* That moment provided me with the best laugh of the day. I actually had an opportunity to have a mini dialogue with my Defensive Self, and it went like this.

"What is the big deal about the blender?"

The shake is going to fly out and splash all over the kitchen!

"Okay, if you feel that might happen, all we need to do is turn it off. Is it really worth it for you to get so upset and uptight about a blender? You're making yourself crazy and the solution is very simple: take a breath, relax, and put a smile on your face. Nothing bad happened. Let's have the shake, it tastes wonderful."

The moral of the story is we all have to coach, relax, reassure and support our Defensive Self so it can relax and become more at peace with life, be less threatened, and less reactive. It is quite a job, but it's our loving responsibility towards ourselves. At the same time, it is very important to let our Emotional Self out of the box and give that part of ourselves playtime.

Do yourself a favor. Find what it means to you, and schedule a bit of heaven on a daily basis.

WRITING REFLECTION

_____

_____

_____

Committed To Grace

Years ago, I visited The Met to see the Interwoven Globe exhibit. The exhibit tells the story of human passion for the art and craft of beautiful fabric and the shared exchange of inspiration between east and west. My eyes were bathing in the exquisite colors and shapes of these inspirationally woven and painted fabrics. It was a moment immersed in beauty.

Next to me was an elderly lady in her late 80s. She was walking slowly, leaning on her cane. As I moved passed her, she looked at me and smiled. Her eyes were full of tremendous light. She was radiating grace. She just smiled and moved on, but my heart stopped. The love, joy, and warmth of her eyes struck me. All of the sudden, at that moment, the saying, "Seeing God in the eyes of others" became an unshakable experience. "She is committed to grace," I thought to myself.

I'm sure she had her share of disappointments, hardships, and challenges, but it seemed to me that her soul returned, over and over again, to grace. My senses told me that she had moved through the "darkness" as a passage for gathering strength so that she could embrace more of the light. That one smile and that one moment taught me what a life of a commitment to grace could make possible.

Our light is born out of darkness. Every negative situation is a stone on the road to enlightenment. If we learn to walk over through negativity and transform those lessons learned into tools of empowerment, then we'll also be able to smile with the grace of God in our eyes.

Let's take an example: Think of a challenging situation in your life. You might have an emotional reaction; pain, anger, fear. Let yourself feel your emotions, but at the same time remember that you are not your feelings. You have them, but you are not them. You might also have a defensive reaction. The most important thing here is to tap into the compassion and awareness that lives in our inner wisdom. Look at every situation through the lens of your Expanded Self, with that vision; you will always facilitate clarity and empowerment, since you will be seated at the seat of grace.

WRITING REFLECTION

_____

_____

_____

The You Behind Yourself

We all get hypnotized by and engrossed in the events of our daily life. Our Defensive Self is continuously on guard, watching out for problems, painful situations, and possible failures. It feels like it must be ready and able to tackle both life's little and big disasters. God knows it finds the "danger" even where it does not exist. It is persistently on edge, worried, and trying to maintain control.

On the other hand, our Emotional Self is full of emotional reactions. It feels joy looking at a beautiful sky; it is upset watching a child crying, horrified by an accident on the road, and tickled by a lover's text message, all within one hour. It is continuously thrown from one emotion to the next like a child would.

As you can see, there is a tremendous amount of commotion going on inside of us every moment. These two aspects of ourselves, our Defensive Self and Emotional Self, are very reactive and are identified with the "drama" of life. Thank God that we have the third aspect, our Expanded Self, the witness who can compassionately and peacefully observe the drama and not get entangled in it. It can watch the movie of our lives and know that it is not the movie. It is not the events, circumstances, or the interpretations.

Our Expanded Self knows itself as pure awareness, peaceful and all knowing. This is the essence of you: your True Self, beyond the body, mind, and personal reactions. Rest yourself as much as possible. Sit in the big armchair of your Expanded Self and watch your Emotional and Defensive Selves. Peacefully and gently, guide and relax them. One day, you will find that they too will pull their little chairs and sit by you, joining the peace, and what a relief that would be.

LET THE HEART SPEAK

WRITING REFLECTION

_____

_____

_____

Are You On Your Life Path?

This is another question that clients often ask me. I also hear it from friends and acquaintances. Here are some helpful tips to answer this question:

1. Your true life path incorporates your gifts, talents, and abilities.

2. Your life path feels natural, and you have a feeling that you belong there, even in spite of difficulties or challenges. The level of comfort may vary from person to person; some people may feel fully comfortable, while others may feel awkward and nervous, but still know that it's the right place for them. You may find yourself thinking or saying, "Yes, this is what I'm supposed to be doing."

3. Your life path brings you deep satisfaction and a sense of fulfillment, even when you are struggling with obstacles and setbacks.

4. Your life path is not something that you do to impress, look good, please your parents, achieve status or money, prove your worth, or get acknowledged. These traits of our defensive self might be mixed in since we are human, but they are not the propelling force behind choosing a true life path.

5. Your life path gives you the opportunity to share your talents and abilities with others, and it feels good to do so.

6. Your life path is aligned with your spiritual and emotional evolution, as well as with your spiritual path.

Thinking about these indicators and reflecting on how you're spending your days can give you valuable insight as to whether you are aligned with your life path or not.

WRITING REFLECTION

Your Life Is A Contribution

The universe seems to be purposeful, initiating constant change, growth, and evolution. We witness its purposeful motion in nature and in our lives. The energy and consciousness within an apple seed propels and guides it to grow into a flowering plant. The same energy and consciousness propel an embryo to develop, a child to grow into an adult, and a creative project to manifest into reality. The human soul is also a seed. Its purpose is to grow into a powerful tree expressing the Creator's consciousness. Just like one apple seed can bring forth a tree with hundreds of apples over many years, a single human soul can inspire and enlighten generations of humanity. There are many varieties of apples. In the same way, each of us is a unique soul, and we fulfill our purpose in diverse and original ways. At the same time, we all share the same purpose, which is to realize and actualize our true nature.

One of the most important lessons is expressing the best of us in the reality of our daily living. It is through our humanity that we express our spiritual nature. It sounds contradictory, but it is really complementary. Knowing what is your personal way of fulfilling your purpose is not an intellectual understanding; it is a deep, intuitive experience, and it is coupled with a desire to share and contribute.

Each one of your talents is a contribution waiting to happen, and an experience of joy. Your life path should include all the things that are truly important and fulfilling to you. If family is important to you, then it is part of your life path. If you are passionate about creating a successful business, it is part of your life path. If you are an artist, it is in your life path. Each one of us has a few important elements that are woven together to create our life path. All elements should be honored and given energy and attention. Of course, it is a balancing act. It takes skills and commitment to keep all elements flourishing at the same time. Family, relationships and work/contribution are three of the main elements. The fourth element can be our spiritual and emotional growth while the fifth can be learning, discovery, and travel. There are other elements. Each one of our paths is a unique combination of elements. We are the weavers of our life's tapestry according to our needs, passions, desires, and abilities. By actively creating our life, we enrich our soul, inspire and support others, and enhance all creation.

WRITING REFLECTION

_____

_____

_____

Being In The Moment

There are times in our lives when our usual hectic-ness rises to its highest levels. Last month was one of those times for me. There were sleepless nights, construction dust, noise, commotion, jury duty, and many important projects that were calling out to me, in need of my much-divided attention.

My meditation time was reduced to a sliver and my peace of mind was thrown out the window. I needed an emergency dose of being in the moment: breathing and just enjoying. So last weekend, I took myself to the waterfront by the Hudson and sat on a bench, classical music pouring into my frazzled mind from my iPod. I released my long list of things to do, things to think about, "should," and "what if's." Intentionally and deliberately, I emptied my mind's cramped space. It took a while.

Then, I started gazing at the clouds and their awe-striking beauty, mystery, colors and shapes. I watched their ever-changing and slowly drifting journeys. I listened to the cries of the seagulls. I heard the wind whispering in the trees, playing with the swaying branches. The unbridled joy of kids and dogs playing brought a smile to my heart.

I was letting it all flow through me, intertwined with the music of Bach in my ears. I was growing wider and wider inside, slowly opening and dissolving into the sweetness of the moment.

As I walked back home, my mind lingered with an appreciation for the sunset. The road back home welcomed me back to me. Our peace is just a moment away if we reach out for it.

WRITING REFLECTION

Transparency And Your Life

The poetic, ecstatic, and inspiring moments of our lives are born out of our ability to feel.

Transparency is something that is not encouraged in our social-political culture, workspace, or the official conducts of government. The lack of transparency creates a blockage in a culture's emotional and spiritual energy flow. It is not benefitting us as individuals or as a society. Lack of transparency creates distrust, frustration, and anger. Most importantly, it accommodates the lack of integrity and prevents creative and positive forward movement.

WRITING REFLECTION

_____

_____

_____

Ask Yourself
The 4 Grand Questions

All knowledge, art, science, philosophy, etc. investigates and expresses our understanding of reality. We, humans, seem to have an insatiable thirst for delving into the mysteries of the universe. We yearn to express its beauty and participate with its creative ever inventing force. The Gate of Knowledge, one of the seven gates in the Gates of Power® Method, supports your personal inquiry into the nature of reality and encourages you to make a commitment to a continuous and consistent learning, questioning, and understanding.

Each one of us has their favorite areas of life which we like to understand and express. Since all paths lead to the truth, much like all rivers yearn to return to the ocean; it does not matter which area you're passionate about. If you feel and contemplate any area deeply and earnestly, you will inevitably touch its truth and slowly come to know it. The main thing is to keep asking, learning, and opening up to gaining a deeper knowledge of self, others, and life.

On our journey of discovery, we ask these five questions.

1. Who am I?
2. Why am I here?
3. What's in my way?
4. How do I get there?

I'm going to touch on these questions a little bit.

"**Who am I?**" Here is a quote from one of my beloved teachers, Shri Brahmananda Sarasvati. "Every living being has at the same time the individual 'I-am' and the cosmic 'I-Am' or the individual self and cosmic self. The cosmic self is beyond the body and mind, beyond gender, beyond all character sign and symbol. The cosmic 'I-Am' is real and the individual 'I-am' is its reflection or shadow. The reflected 'I-am' has two choices to identify with the body and mind on the one side or to identify with the cosmic 'I-Am' on the other side. In reality, this individual 'I-am' is the image of the cosmic 'I-Am' and when we know and feel that, the individual 'I-am' becomes the cosmic "I-Am."

"Why am I here?" What comes to my mind is that we're here to realize the truth of who we are and to participate as co-creators with the universal mind.

"What's in my way?" Identifying with ourselves as finite beings creates fear. Fear creates defensiveness and defensiveness contracts and limits our consciousness.

"How do I get there?" Using our expanding awareness, understanding the truth about ourselves, others, and life, and by the consistent and committed daily work on our self-evolution, we can take ourselves to where we are meant to be.

Reflection Pause: Have you asked yourself these questions before? Even if you did, take a minute to revisit them again and write down some of your thoughts.

WRITING REFLECTION

_____

_____

_____

What Is The Universe Made Of?

On July 4, 2012 scientists at CERN announced that they found a particle that behaved the way they expect the Higgs Boson to act. Its nickname is the "God particle." The intriguing possibility is that the Higgs Boson is responsible for all the mass in the universe. The theory is that all particles have no inherent mass, but instead gain mass as they pass through a field. This field is known as the Higgs field. Is it possible that this confirms the ancient knowledge that the universe is consciousness transforming into energy and vice-versa?

WRITING REFLECTION

_____

_____

_____

Lack Of Awareness: The Cost

The most precious gift we have as human beings is our ability to be aware. It gives us the power to witness our thoughts, feelings, and actions and to meditate about them, learn lessons and evolve.

The earth, including the plant and animal kingdom, operates instinctively guided by the laws of nature. Man has the privilege of guiding his/her actions, thoughts and feelings.

WRITING REFLECTION

_____

_____

_____

Seven Ways To Thank Your Body

Whenever we start a new cycle, it is wise to take care of the basic elements of living. By doing this, we create a sense of grounding, which allows for our spirit and our emotions to soar freely. Our body, the temple of our inner being, is the most important of this basic element. By taking care of it, we create a peaceful and balanced home for our spirit. Let's start by thanking our body for being there and serving us:

1. The Smile
Every morning as soon as you wake up, stretch! Make it a wide juicy stretch with sounds, accompanied with a big smile. Then thank your body for bringing you another day full of possibilities, adventures, and enjoyment.

2. The Touch.
Touch your cheeks, your shoulders, your tummy or any parts of the body you choose. Acknowledge them for the work they have done for you. Be specific. Example: "Thank you hands for writing, washing dishes, helping with yoga poses, hugging, and bringing my favorite health bar to my mouth!"

3. The Song.
When you step into the shower, cover your body with some sweet-smelling soap and sing a little song of joy and praise. Go ahead and invent a melody. Have fun!

4. The Beauty Treat.
Pour some wonderfully silky lotion on your loyal servant…your body, and give it a gentle healing massage.

5. The Taste.
When you make your breakfast, tune into what it is that your body

wants to eat on that particular day. Don't just give it the usual. Make it interesting, a little different. Your body needs variety and adventure.

6. Time to Move.
Allow the body some expression. How about putting some great music on? Take 10 minutes to "Boogie." It is the best way to give your body "joy" time.

7. The Color.
Getting dressed, ask yourself, "What does my body feel comfortable in this morning? What are the colors and textures for today?" Put on clothes that would make your **BODY** and **YOU** happy. Each day is different. Celebrate it with a fresh combination of colors and textures.

Take time to love the precious container of your spirit. It will send much love back. Because thanking our body helps it to relax and heal.

Enjoy!

WRITING REFLECTION

_____

_____

_____

Your Daily Dose Of Happiness

Our days are filled with work and worry. Our "To Do List" is so comprehensive that most of the time, we forget to do the small things for ourselves. Like the vitamins, our parents told us to take every day; we need to remember to give our inner being its daily vitamins as well. Think of them as supplements of happiness or as I like to think of it- as my favorite, joy pills. Below are some things that have helped me and I hope they help you as well, Enjoy!

Lazy Time

Lazy time was definitely one of the most difficult things for me to get used to. Just thinking about it got me anxious; the overachiever in me would panic. If you are like me, lazy time is a must. I always admired people who could lounge around, being deliciously lazy for hours. I also used to think that they were wasting their life away. I had a love-hate relationship to laziness. Later, I realized that laziness, like most things in life, needs to be kept in balance. A person also needs to assess why he or she is lazy. Is it because they need rest, or are they using it to avoid something? The lazy time I am suggesting is a conscious choice to rest, relax, and replenish. This doing nothing is not an avoidance tactic but a pause, an energetic slowdown, a full permission to let go of doing and thinking. Lazy time is on my personal list of pleasures. Check with yourself—are you resting or are you avoiding? Do you allow yourself some lazy time or are you compulsively doing, doing, doing, and more? It's a question of balance, giving and receiving, inhaling and exhaling.

Using Your Hands to Create

There are many ways to enjoy creating things with your hands. You must admit that it is satisfying to see the end results of these creative activities. Start by looking around the house for possibilities. For example, I painted patterns of red and gold inside all of my lampshades to achieve a certain atmosphere, and I love it. I created an angel out of strings of gold and silver wires and gemstones to put above my bed. I had never done that before, and never since. I created earrings and necklaces, changed or added fabric on my decorative pillows, and the list goes on. Get your hands busy. Repaint a picture frame or a room. Cook, knit, build a bookshelf, or mount one. Rearrange the furniture, mend the broken chair, and give it a new look. Clear the closets and re-organize or renew their compartments. Repot plants. These simple, creative projects are "doing" meditations. They quiet the mind and enhance your environment.

Delight in Being

Choose a day and dedicate it to indulging in your senses. On that day, commit to experiencing all your regular daily activities with extra-open senses. For example, noticing how the light hits your eyes first thing in the morning. How your body feels under the covers. How does that first step out of bed feel? The water on your face? The sounds of the street? The taste of your first cup of tea or coffee? This is a great practice in being present in the moment and present to your senses. It teaches you to appreciate being alive. You will be distracted. Don't let it discourage you. Keep coming back to your senses.

Your joy pills might be different from mine, but what is important is that you give yourself these indulgences daily. Do remember to take these in conjunction with your "healthy pleasures." If you don't feel better after, feel free to call me in the morning.

WRITING REFLECTION

_____

_____

_____

Healthy Pleasures

One of my favorite healthy pleasures is recalling at the end of a day my magic moments and my tiny or substantial victories. I highly recommend doing this. Reliving a magical moment or acknowledging a victory replenishes your trust in yourself and the goodness and beauty of life. A magic moment can happen when you are looking at the moon or sunset. It can happen when you are playing with a child, giggling with your friends, or feeling playful at work for no reason. It could be a moment in a movie, at a concert, in nature, or on the subway. A magic moment can happen anywhere, anytime. It is up to us to be available, still, and open enough to experience it. Acknowledging our victories enhances our ability to create more of them. Getting to a yoga class, when you didn't feel like going, is a victory. Being able to work through a reactive feeling without attacking or shutting down is a great victory. Saying no when it's difficult but appropriate, or saying yes when you feel like running away. Speaking your mind in a meeting or an important conversation is a victory. Taking a bath when you need it in spite of more work that needs to be done, is a victory for the overachiever. Doing work into the night when it is a must, in spite of your lazy tendency is a victory. The list is long. We're not used to acknowledging ourselves for the so-called little victories (or even for the big ones). All victories count; they all give us strength.

The List of Healthy Pleasures:

1. Start by listing all things that give you pleasure (healthy pleasure as opposed to destructive; I hope you can tell the difference). You should be able to list at least twenty things. Here are some suggestions. Foods, activities, movies, music, books, arts, crafts, travel, play, sports, working out, dancing, lovemaking, sleeping, baths, singing, laughing, surfing the net, the beach, and the mountains, etc.

2. Include in your list what would also be fun to do if you dared to be out of your comfort zone. Some example, skydiving, belly dancing, drumming, rollerblading, scuba diving, rock climbing, dressing up for Halloween, and karaoke.

3. Make your bucket list. List all the things you would like to do before you pass out of this world. The list may include places you'd like to visit, projects you want to accomplish, skills you want to cultivate, people you want to meet, and experiences you want to have.

Look at all these three lists and commit to doing at least one of your pleasures a day. Make sure you vary your pleasures to cover all three lists. Pleasure is good for your soul and for your looks. It puts a smile in your heart and moves the chi in your body.

Go for it.

WRITING REFLECTION

_____

_____

_____

Your Partners, Your Team, Your Life

Think about the things in your life that you enjoy and cherish most. How many of these do you do with others? We are partnering all the time. Life is a big canvas of teamwork, giving and receiving.

Exercise:

Write down all the partnerships in your life. The list of partners can be anyone. For example, you may write any of the following: My spouse, my parents (each one is a partnership), my kids, my siblings, my friends, my jazz group, my tennis partner, my doctor, my accountant, my students, and so on.

Look at your list. As you can see, your life is rich with partnerships of all kinds. Each partner brings out something different in you, and each partner gives you something unique. There is a constant exchange of knowledge, love, support, fun, and challenge. Partnerships keep you growing and giving. People who know how to respect and enjoy their partnerships evolve faster and achieve more. To manifest your life vision, you need to be a good team player, a good partner. You need to inspire and be inspired. You need to give and enjoy receiving. You need to reach out and be there for another. You need to discover and create with others. Our power lies in our ability to relate and partner with ourselves and others. The three central aspects of yourself are a partnership, and when this union is solid, you are centered.

Reflections pause:

Take a look at your partnering abilities. Even though we feel and behave a little differently within each partnership, we can still notice general tendencies. What kind of a partner are you, in general? Here are some questions to ask yourself: Am I a generous or a reserved partner? Am I expressive and honest or am I inauthentic? Am I a team player or do I need to be in the center, making my partners my audience? Do I know how to listen? Do I easily get defensive? Do I respect my partners? Do I show appreciation? Do I support and encourage, or am I quick to analyze, criticize, and judge? Do I love cooperation or am I a loner? Etc.

I hope you got an honest picture of your partnering style. If it is not optimal—then none of us can honestly say that we have mastered the art of partnering—we have to get to work. Realize that who you are as a partner (to yourself, as well as to others) shapes who you are and affects your destiny.

WRITING REFLECTION

_____

_____

_____

Communication Is Key

If we are to survive and thrive, we have to work together. All the signs are pointing us in that direction. Each one of us needs to take responsibility for our inner development and together, as a people, we need to take mutual responsibility for global development. This calls for a connection between all individuals and nations to gain a greater unity.

Change starts at home. Let's start by looking at our communication with the people we are close too. Are we honest? Are we compassionate? Are we authentic? Are we supportive?

Not always…we should all develop our communication skills and cultivate supportive relationships.

Here are some guidelines for positive communication:

- **Observing as opposed to judging.** Most of us find it hard to make observations without rushing to make judgments. We tend to immediately and, at times, unconsciously categorize or misshape what we are observing. We need to cultivate compassionate witnessing, without rushing to evaluate or judge.

- **Identifying our feelings and needs.** When we know what we feel and what we need, because we have taken the time to be with our feelings and defined our needs, we can communicate them better.

- **Expressing ourselves clearly and honestly.** This is always a challenge. What can help us is accepting our subjective reality and expressing our experience without blaming, pointing the finger, or attacking the other person. This is not always easy to do, but it is a very crucial skill for one to have.

- **Requesting as opposed to not asking or demanding.** When we need something from another, a close friend, a colleague or an acquaintance, it is more effective to request what we need rather than not saying anything or demanding.

- **Listening emphatically to others.** Cultivating true listening skills is a cornerstone of communication. This involves taking the time to listen, listening from the heart and putting ourselves in another person's shoes.

- **Mirroring.** This is the skill of reflecting back to another person what we heard them express, showing them that we understood them.

- **Giving and receiving appreciation.** We all need appreciation and acknowledgment. It is imperative to open ourselves up to receiving appreciation, as well as offering it to others.

These guidelines are not easy to master, but practicing them is well worth it. These skills enrich our lives, as well as the lives of others.

WRITING REFLECTION

_____

_____

_____

Live In The Moment

Mindfulness is the art of attention and awareness. It lives in the present moment, which is the only moment we have. It is a form of non-judgmental, relaxed awareness. When we are mindful, we are consciously paying attention on purpose to the contents of each moment. We are noticing our feelings and sensations. We are taking in the details of our external environment, as well as the emotional and mental currents that are flowing within us. Mindfulness also means cultivating a relaxed acceptance of what is. We learn to allow what happens to just "be" and observe it with compassion. We are witnessing rather than resisting, controlling or fixing.

Sounds easy? Not at all. Mindfulness takes tremendous practice since we all are, to various degrees, anxious and reactive. We tend to live in the past, or in the future, going back and forth from one to the other in an effort, mostly unconscious, to manipulate life and outsmart it. Just being in the present moment feels very open and vulnerable. Most of us are too restless to relax into the moment. We end up being absent from our own life, a guest rather than the homeowner.

Isn't it interesting that we forget that we are here in this life temporarily? We might not be here tomorrow. Our moments are precious, but we're not living them fully. We are doing things automatically, unconsciously, taking life for granted. Mindfulness reduces stress and enhances our ability to enjoy and appreciate life. It opens our hearts and minds to an expanded experience of life, and relaxes our tendency to contract and withdraw away from what is.

WRITING REFLECTION

_____

_____

_____

Silence And Meditation: Resting Your Mind

In these hectic times we live in, times of quick and disturbing changes, times of turbulence and shifts in consciousness, it is paramount to devote ourselves to a practice of stillness, on a daily basis. By so doing, we wash away the noise, drama, and distractions of the world and tap into a state of peace and oneness.

Use the silence to reach the highest and the best in you.

What is silence? This seemingly simple question could be answered thus: silence is the absence of noise. Sometimes in the middle of the night, one might wake up and hear silence. The world is quiet.

But there is another kind of silence that is rare and hard to tune into—a deep stillness inside in which you hear eternity. You feel a peaceful merging with all that is. In this inner quiet, you experience yourself melting, expanding and dissolving as if you are losing and finding yourself all at once. Time stops, or maybe it stretches, and all that you think you know disappears into a yet deeper knowing. Your personal river of energy finds the sea. A great, sweet calmness comes over you, and you embrace it like a lover finding a long lost love. That is the silence of the soul.

In that sanctuary, we feel the pulse of life and the presence of the One. This is a place of true knowledge beyond words and thoughts. Some people who engage in meditation and who have experienced the beauty of this state cannot wait to be there again and again, and the ones that have mastered it walk within the rattling, restless world cloaked in peace.

LET THE HEART SPEAK

Why is it that it seems like we do everything possible to avoid this nurturing peace? The quiet seems to scare us. Does the stillness confront us with all that we have not yet faced? We keep running from ourselves—through overdoing, over-chatting, overbuying, overeating, over-fighting, etc.—to numb the truth. The very truth, which despite all its possibly painful shades, sets us free if we can walk into its flames and pass through them.

Do you allow yourself stillness? By that, I mean a time when you're doing nothing and resting your mind, just breathing and being present? If your answer is no, or not enough, the Gate of Silence is an invitation to cultivate a practice of stillness and mindfulness.

WRITING REFLECTION

_____

_____

_____

Living Creatively

"What does it mean exactly to live creatively?" you might be asking.

The first thing I want to say is that it does not mean that you have to be an artist or necessarily create anything that falls into the category of artwork. It means to live intimately close to your childlike nature, your Emotional Self. Even when it is pained by unresolved past experiences, your Emotional Self longs for creative expression. It loves adventures. It loves nature. And it is up for fun and silliness, if given the permission and the opportunity.

Our creative and expressive nature endures many blows, starting in childhood. We are told not to cry like babies when we are only two or three years old. We're told to sit still, stop giggling, stop being silly, stop screaming, stop singing, and stop making faces, etc. In other words, the message is stop having a good time. Stop experiencing your feelings. Early on, our ability to live creatively begins to diminish. We must learn to be "good." We cannot take the risk of losing love, so we begin to cultivate our Defensive Self, which means our tactics for survival. If being expressive and creative is not approved, we learn to repress it. Slowly and surely, we forget the feeling of expressive freedom. We comply with our parents' demands and expectations. Then, we comply with those of teachers, peers, bosses, lovers, neighbors, and even strangers. We learn to be what we are expected to be. We learn that it is important to get ahead, make money, raise a family, and be responsible. There is nothing in this script that tells us to "be ourselves."

One of my clients came to see me because his marriage was falling apart. He asked me, "Being myself. What is that? Who knows? Where do I find that self, and why should I?" Lack of intimate communication was his wife's complaint. "I'm doing everything for the family...

making good money, getting ahead. I'm responsible and loyal. What does she want?" he wondered. "She wants to hear your feelings. She wants to tell you about hers," I said. "I don't know what my feelings are," he told me. "Feelings about what?" he asked. This very kind and truly responsible man had buried his Emotional Self so deeply that it took a long and much-needed archaeological dig to find it and resurrect it. Your Emotional Self is the one who can bring in the enjoyment, vulnerability, and love that you need.

Most of us are reluctant to experience the intensity of our feelings. We know that underneath the surface of safe emotions, there are layers of difficult and possibly painful ones. Naturally, we resist them, but when we don't feel deeply, we don't heal, and we don't find that lost self through which we experience and enjoy life. To me, living creatively means allowing ourselves to rediscover and express our Emotional Self in all its colors and states. Painful, silly, loving, outrageous, innocent, angry, and curious.

This is a tricky process. We descend into scary realms, we grieve, we release, we soar, we give birth to ourselves, and we learn to be. It is also a creative process that teaches us courage and inspires us to keep living life as an adventure.

WRITING REFLECTION

_____

_____

_____

The Three Gifts

We are blessed with three precious gifts bestowed on us by the Creative Source.

1. Freedom to choose the way we lead our lives.

2. The ability to create and express.

3. The desire to give and receive love.

Can you think of three more important elements? These gifts are ours, free of charge. We seldom stop to acknowledge these gifts and be grateful for them. We take them for granted. A person's life is measured by the way he or she is using these three gifts. Take a minute and evaluate how you honor these in your life. Ask yourself:

How am I using my free will? Am I taking full responsibility for my choices? Am I making choices that lead me to growth and fulfillment? Or Am I keeping myself limited and confined?

Take a look at your choices from the small ones of what you eat and how you exercise to the big ones of how you walk your life path or how you relate to yourself and others. An honest and compassionate examination can propel you to shift some of your choices and possibly commit deeper to the best in you. Now do the same with the question of:

How are you using the gift of your creativity and authentic expression?

Are you hiding behind a mask, playing a role or are you taking chances on being creative and expressive. Last but not least:

LET THE HEART SPEAK

How are you managing your heart? Are you dedicated to have a loving attitude towards yourself and others? Or are you sheltered behind defensive walls, playing it safe?

You and I know that the journey of life is not colored black and white. We live in the grey, inching forward consciously and consistently towards our openness. What matters is our commitment to actualizing these three most beautiful gifts we were given.

WRITING REFLECTION

_____

_____

_____

The Origin Of Stress

On Monday, February 13th, I was lecturing a group of mothers, and the topic was "The Origin of Stress and How to Alleviate It." When we started getting to the root of the issue, I asked the group these questions:

"What are the origins of stress?"

These were some of the answers- worry, time constraints, finance, physical, emotional, and spiritual pressures.

When we examined these, we discovered that we produce stress by putting pressure on ourselves. We resist our feelings, denying and repressing them. We are overly demanding harsh and critical towards ourselves, and we are careless regarding our true needs. Ultimately, stress is a result of lack of true self-care. I then asked the second question, "You are all dedicated mothers but:

"Are you mothering yourselves"?

As we discovered in our discussion, most of us are not doing a great job in taking care of ourselves; and we all should. The better mothering we provide for ourselves, the better mothering we're able to extend to our children and loved ones.

I continued by explaining in my method, Gates of Power® Method and defining three aspects that compromise our inner being:

1. **The Emotional Self**

2. **The Defensive Self**

3. **The Expanded Self**

The emotional part of ourselves is repressed and criticized by our survival-oriented and over-protective Defensive Self. The Defensive Self is trying hard to "make us" loveable, successful, and perfect. It is trying to compensate for lack of self-esteem and emotional vulnerability. Naturally, it is more concerned with our image and others' approval of us, rather than with our well-being. Doing so, it ends up stressing us. Our Expanded Self, the third aspect, is the wise, loving and healing aspect. It is the one that should lead our lives. In the Gates Of Power® Method, participants learn to access their Expanded Self and use its skills to relax the Defensive Self and free the Emotional Self. In other words, ideally, the Expanded Self should be the parent, coach and guide of the other two. We all must learn the art and the craft of inner parenting to establish real peace and balance. We are better communicators when we communicate lovingly with ourselves.

WRITING REFLECTION

_____

_____

_____

A Loving Good-Bye To Whitney Houston

This section was written in February of 2012 in response to the untimely death of Whitney Houston.

Whitney was a great artist, a beautiful person, and a loving human being who lost the battle to stress and addiction. In my last section, I spoke about the origin of stress. Here is a summary of some of the elements that cause stress in us:

- Low self-esteem
- Unresolved inner conflicts, inner pain, and trauma
- Repressed feelings
- Chronic habit of worry and anxiety
- Lack of trust in one's self and the direction of one's life
- Critical harsh or shaming self-dialogue
- Poor communication skills
- Poor organization and management skills
- Poor management of commitments, time, physical, financial, and social goal and obligations.

We are all prone to stress. It is inevitable. However, we can reduce it by becoming aware of what is stressing us and making a conscious effort to eliminate as much of it as possible. For the first three elements on the list, it will take emotional, psychological, and spiritual work to undo the stress. The most basic and important element is resolving inner conflicts, inner pain, and trauma. When these are resolved, it boosts our self-esteem. We learn to appreciate and respect ourselves. In the process, repressed feelings are released and resolved.

Once we gain a better self-image and a higher self-esteem, we can begin to let go of the habit of worry. We learn to trust ourselves and the direction of our life. Our self-dialogue improves, and we're ready to enhance our communication and organization skills.

Unfortunately, a lot of us are not willing to do the work it takes to shift and empower our state of being. Instead, we reach out to easier solutions, which are sometimes addictions. We might use substances like food, drugs, and alcohol; or non-substance addictions like relationships, work, TV, sex, and sleep etc. Addictions create the illusion of comfort. However, this comfort is temporary………we always need more.

Addictions are progressive diseases that will eventually kill our spirit, destroy our body, strain our relationships and rob us of the life we were supposed to lead. The power to heal and free ourselves lies within us, and we need to learn how to tap into and utilize it. It is both our responsibility and gift to ourselves.

WRITING REFLECTION

_____

_____

_____

Loving Communications: The Ten Commandments

Giving and receiving love is the most nourishing and life affirming exchange. It is the spiritual gold currency that makes the world go round.

I would like to suggest the following Ten Commandments. They will help you to communicate better. Good communication, as we all know, is a key to creating a loving exchange:

1. **Know yourself.** Find out how you feel, what you need, and what you believe in, so that you can communicate it.

2. **Commit to creating connections.** Take responsibility for the success of your communications. Be the cause, the initiator, the giver.

3. **Avoid reactivity.** When faced with strong emotions and intense reactions, take a minute to figure yourself out. Get clear and strive to create a constructive way to communicate.

4. **Cultivate empathic listening.** Extend this empathy to yourself and others. Empathy helps you understand and accept. It enhances transformation and change.

5. **Be clear**. Be authentic and expressive, and use the four "Magic I's." (I Think, I Feel, I Need, I Want). When you communicate with another, stick to expressing your feelings rather than pointing the finger at the other. Avoid blaming, dumping, judging or telling others what to do.

6. **Show appreciation.** Do whatever you can to validate your partner(s). Use listening and mirroring skills, show respect and consideration. You can still maintain your beliefs while maintaining such an approach. One has nothing to do with the other.

7. **Be reliable.** Say what you mean and mean what you say. Integrity cultivates mutual trust.

8. **Learn to negotiate.** Create win-win situations. It is best for all involved.

9. **Tap into your humor and playfulness.** Bring enjoyment into your communications.

10. **Let go of the need to be right, in control, or on top.** Connection and the exchange of understanding are so much more fulfilling.

Communication is an art. Keep experimenting and go through the trials and tribulations. You will come to enjoy it and your loved ones will appreciate it too.

WRITING REFLECTION

_____

_____

_____

The Manifestation Highway

As I promised you in the last section, I will share with you a practical and inspiring process to ensure that you manifest your goals, and your dreams. You will have to do the work that each step presents, but if you do, you will move forward without a doubt. I have defined a seven step process that I call "The Manifestation Highway."

Remember each step builds off the last. No shortcuts on this highway!

Here are the steps:

1. Positive Inner Paradigm
2. Vision
3. Road Map
4. Choices
5. Committed Positions
6. Forward Motion
7. Celebration of Victories

Positive Inner Paradigm

This step is the most important one; if we do not create a positive view of yourself, others and life in general, we will not manifest success. Most of us get stuck in this step. In the Gates of Power Method® we work towards a deep appreciation of self, others, and life. Out of that positive soil, healthy desires and dreams grow.

Vision

In this step, we cultivate a clear vision that springs out of our deepest passions, needs, and desires. The vision needs to be detailed and specific. We need to be able to imagine ourselves living, doing, and feeling whatever we see in our vision.

Roadmap/Plan

This step is about making a plan of action. The plan should be well thought out, practical, and specific. We need to chart our steps, include deadlines and desired results.

Choices

We have our vision. We have our roadmap. Now it's time to prioritize and make clear choices. Each step on the plan requires us to make specific choices that will translate into actions.

Commitments

Once we have defined our choices, we need to make a list of commitments that will serve our choices. Our commitments need to also be specific. "How many by when!" which means how many are we going to do, and by what time and date?

Actions/Forward Motion

Now, it's time to take action. We have the list of our commitments and we have to act upon them consistently with focus and discipline. If we find that certain actions don't bring us the results that we desire, we need to shift and possibly make new choices preceded by commitments and actions. We keep our eye on the vision, and no matter how many times we fall, we get up and wipe the dust off our pants and keep walking.

Celebration of Victories

We acknowledge even the smallest of victories, and we allow

ourselves to feel a sense of gratitude and joy about achieving them. We also acknowledge our team and anyone that has supported us in getting there.

WRITING REFLECTION

_____

_____

_____

Mastering Success

Making New Year's resolutions is exciting. We get inspired motivated and filled with hope. It's a little like falling in love. We envision ourselves fit, healthy, and full of vitality. We envision a life of friendships, great relationships, and adventures. We envision ourselves taking bold steps moving forward on our life path. Life is full of promise. All is well.

Then the daily routine sets in with its tide of unproductive habits, self-doubts, fears and resistance. The overwhelming list of our chores, errands, duties, bills and obligations begins to flood our consciousness and drain our energy. By the end of January, all of the amazing "New Year's Resolution Energy" is dissipated and life feels somewhat grey, dull and uninspiring. It feels as if we fell out of love.

We begin to experience a sense of disappointment, a familiar feeling of letting ourselves down. The truth is that we need a process and a discipline to help us move from resolutions to implementation. Without it, our dreams stay just that- dreams. Falling in love is great, falling out of love feels like a loss, but the true key is learning how to love. In the same way having a dream is great, losing a dream is disappointing, but the key is learning how to realize your dreams.

WRITING REFLECTION

_____

_____

_____

A Note On Self Love: Small Steps To Rehab

This section was written in July of 2011 in response to Amy Winehouse's unfortunate passing.

Last weekend was especially heartbreaking for the staff and me at Gates of Power. We learned the tragic news of the death of beloved singer and songwriter, Amy Winehouse, as many of you did. And it was the words of her hit song "Rehab" that struck us as a poignant demonstration of how she and so many we encounter miss the most vital ingredient needed for true rehabilitation – a transformation of the heart.

The greatest tragedy of Amy rested not only in her unfortunate and premature passing. What makes her young tormented life, and ultimately, her death, so tremendously unfortunate, is that both were the result of a soul devoid of authentic and lasting self-love. Had she gone to rehabilitation for substance abuse- yes; she may have had a fighting chance at a better, longer life. But rehab without support, rehab stripped of self-identity, appreciation, and love, is just a faux trapping of an empty being. Such rehabilitation doesn't last. What so many in her position require is a rehabilitation of the soul, a self-embrace and gentle pat on the back of their depleted spirit- taking small steps to self-love rehab.

Most of us find it somewhat uncomfortable to express love and appreciation for ourselves. We were raised to believe that loving ourselves is selfish. The majority of people alive today grew up with parents who were not aware of the power of self-love. Other ideals such as hard work, material success, and education were emphasized. While these were important to convey, the notion of loving-self was omitted, as it was completely foreign to past generations.

This misplaced focus formed a lack of self-worth and underdeveloped self-nurturing skills. The truth is that when you do not truly love and appreciate yourself, you are unable to wholeheartedly accept the gifts of life like, happiness, loving relationships, and even abundance and prosperity. Learning to love yourself is the foundation of all inner work. Such love is the door that allows all dreams and goals to manifest and enter. Your ability to love another person obviously depends on your ability to love yourself. It is the reason loving yourself is not selfish. On the contrary, you become "self-full" – your cup overflows with love, which allows you to share love with others effortlessly.

WRITING REFLECTION

_____

_____

_____

The Importance Of Inner Dialogue

Most of us realize that our close relationships need attention and nurturing. If you are a parent, you do your best to spend quality time with your kids on a daily basis. If you're married, you create time to share with your spouse. And the same goes for close friends, siblings, and parents. Why is it that we don't create the same space and time to commune and communicate with ourselves?

Most of my clients, when they begin working with me, admit that they don't take time to "sit" with themselves. Moreover, they don't know how to do it. I would like to address the importance of having an intimate relationship with oneself. If you cannot understand yourself, you cannot accept yourself; you don't know how to guide yourself, and ultimately, you cannot find love and compassion towards yourself. Disconnection from you means disconnection from others.

To be able to be open, honest, and authentic with others, you have to be able to be that way with yourself. A relationship with oneself, just like any other relationship, needs a consistent investment of time, attention, and care. When I watch the news or observe people who are destructive to themselves and others, it is clear to me that they don't have a caring relationship with themselves. If they did, they wouldn't compromise themselves and the lives of others. Lack of self-care can take many forms: take a minute to think of the ways you are treating yourself or feeling about yourself.

Are you critical, harsh, or rejecting of yourself? Are you neglecting? Are you avoiding your feelings, needs, and desires? Are you disrespecting yourself and allowing others to disrespect you? Ask yourself what needs to be different – what needs to be nurtured?

WRITING REFLECTION

Cultivating Your Personal Relationships

I would guess that if you sat quietly for a few minutes and thought about the three most important things in your life, one of those things would be your relationships with people who are closest to you. If you find that this is true for you, then the next question to ask yourself is: How much do I invest in cultivating these important relationships?

Most of us are extremely busy attempting to handle our personal lives, our career goals, and our social obligations, etc. At times, the people who are most important to us are put on the back burner, not because we don't love or appreciate them, but because we assume they will understand our busy schedule and they will forgive our neglectful tendencies.

I know for sure that unless I schedule a time to talk to my mom, sister, brother, or best friends, there's no time left for them. Other things will come and take that time away. I personally have made a commitment to nurture my close relationships and doing whatever it takes to keep them alive, but sometimes it's not easy. But I realized that these relationships give me the most joy and a valuable sense of support. I am able to speak my heart, to discover my truth, to plan and dream, and share laughter, and be an intimate part of their lives.

Think about the closest person to you and ask yourself how you can better enhance their life right now. It might be three little things that you can do in this next week that would bring a smile to their face. On the other hand, how can you allow them to contribute to you? We all like to give to the people that we love. Are you letting them love you?

WRITING REFLECTION

_____
_____
_____

Life As A Dialogue

All of life is a canvass of dialogue. Within this canvas of energy and consciousness, we are in a constant flow of exchange. We are sustained by an ocean of intelligence and love, nurtured by it and connected through it. Human beings have created a sense of separation. We imagine ourselves to be separate from this nurturing fabric of being. Of course we're not, but by maintaining this sense of separation, we are creating unnecessary suffering for ourselves.

The root of this separation is our disconnection from ourselves, which keeps us separate from others. The tendency of being separate, consciously, or unconsciously, is disempowering and harmful. Unfortunately, it has become socially acceptable and is considered normal. We have developed automatic patterns of living in isolation, which perpetuates our sense of separateness. One of the most important lessons that we have to personally and collectively realize is our connection and unity with others, and with life. Working towards dissolving the sense of separation we have, and creating unity is not an easy task, but it is one of the most urgent ones.

The writing is on the wall, flashing in neon lights. We are all connected. We always were, since the beginning of time. Within the last 50 years, as communication, media, and technology developed, the imagined gap of separateness started closing. The reality of being a global village hit us. We can no longer ignore disasters, corruption or social/political upheavals that are happening on the other side of the globe. We can no longer deny their direct effects on us. There is one matrix of life, and we are all parts of it, interconnected and interdependent. It is time to think, feel and dialogue globally; it is time to open out hearts and minds to our neighbors, our community and beyond, to our world.

Yes, we are very busy – most of us are multitasking – overworked and sometimes overwhelmed. It takes much focus and energy to end a regular day. In spite of all of that, we must get involved and stand up for unity, values, and justice. It is our birthright and our responsibility.

WRITING REFLECTION

_____

_____

_____

Use Your Emotions As A Form Of Contribution

Our feelings are our most precious gift – they allow us to feel the beauty of nature, to empathize with others, to appreciate art and culture, to be moved, inspired, and challenged by life. Become emotionally generous with yourself and others.

Open your heart to the experience of love, by giving and receiving it. Enjoy your moments and appreciate the simple things about life. Share and encourage others to share, acknowledge yourself and others, accept yourself and others, see yourself in others, and cultivate compassion, support, and understanding. The beauty of emotional generosity is that it creates a joy deeper than any other, and a connection that our hearts yearn for the most.

WRITING REFLECTION

_____

_____

_____

Our Emotional Journey

Our emotional journey involves leaving the comfortable and familiar realms to cross over the barriers of fears, and at times, to descend into the valley of what feels like deep despair. Ultimately, we return renewed. The journey can take us to the places that makes us most afraid. Childhood experiences of loneliness, rejection, or betrayal are such to name a few, but it seems like we must revisit these painful places to resolve them, and draw new strength and perspective, which end up as pearls of empowerment, gleaned from the dark waters of hardship. Those who dare to visit these difficult places and have the courage to feel will find a way back to strength and maturity.

Take a minute and be honest with yourself. You might want to write some notes. Ask yourself: How much of my life do I live in the safety of my comfort zone avoiding difficult emotions or situations? If you find that you're doing it a lot, you might want to begin by taking little steps towards changing this habit. Being stuck in a comfort zone is not conducive to personal growth.

WRITING REFLECTION

_____

_____

_____

Celebrate Your Feelings!

Emotions are the glue that binds people to one another. They inspire the human pursuit of beauty, knowledge, and development. Emotions are fundamental to our ability to understand ourselves, each other, and the world. By learning to recognize, honor, and heal your emotions, you become a stronger, more joyous and creative you!

Did you stop for a minute to think of all the important ways your emotions contribute to your life? If you didn't, then THIS IS THE MOMENT!

Here are the ten most obvious ways that your emotions contribute to your life. Your emotions help you:

1. To recognize what makes you happy, what inspires and moves you.
2. To understand yourself and others.
3. To communicate with others.
4. To make decisions.
5. To create your life vision and pursue your goals.
6. To build fulfilling relationships.
7. To create and express.
8. To love, give, and enjoy.
9. To develop and grow.
10. To feel ALIVE!

Let's dedicate today's section to Number 8: Love, Give, and Enjoy. Right now, at this moment (as you read this), acknowledge a few

LET THE HEART SPEAK

things around you and in your life that for which you are very grateful. (For example, it can be your computer, and the fact that it's working!) If you're not listening to music, play something that takes you to a happy place. Enjoy this moment. Forget about your worries and know that at any moment of your choosing, you can tap into the feelings of gratitude and joy!

WRITING REFLECTION

_____

_____

_____

The Body: A Prison Or A Fire Chariot?

Last Saturday, I led a workshop called *The Body: A Prison or a Fire Chariot?* I would like to start by saying that the workshop was an amazing experience for all of us. There was definitely a strong sense of before and after, the after being a much greater sense of freedom, body, mind, and soul for all participants. I want to thank everyone who took part in the workshop for their honesty, authenticity, and support of each other.

Since I have been writing about the Gate of the Body in my last few entries, I want to share with you some details about this workshop. Each participant chose a personal theme that was unresolved and disturbing to them. One of the homework assignments was to meditate, observe their feelings, and write about how this theme affects their body. They were told to sense any muscle tension, tightness, numbness, pain, as well as any physical symptoms, and health issues. By doing this, they were able to define which places in their body were affected by the theme chose. In connection with this exploration, they were also asked to be open to images relating to these places in their bodies.

To illustrate this, I would like to share an experience one participant had. The theme that she chose was an inability to assert herself at times and to create healthy boundaries in her relationships with the people closest to her. She noticed that this theme affected her throat, jaw, and upper shoulders. The image that she got was seeing herself in a very large cave, feeling small. She imagined herself trying to make a sound, but not being able to. In the workshop, she worked on opening up her throat and jaw by making big sounds. At first, these were threatening to her, but later she found joy in the volume of the sound. She also discovered and made gestures with her shoulders and arms that went with the sounds. This is just one example of the many ways we work to open blockages using the body.

A lot of us are afraid to use sounds and authentic movement in our daily life. When we are upset, it is especially important to use sound and movement to allow the upset emotions to express themselves. It helps release the intensity of the feeling and also helps us to understand our feelings better. This way, if we decide to share the feeling, we are coming from a place of clarity rather than reactivity.

WRITING REFLECTION

_____
_____
_____

Freeing The Expression Of The Body

The body and the psyche reflect each other. By freeing the psyche, we free the body and vice versa. I would like to mention some simple and very effective ways to free the soul through freeing the body.

1. Every time we exercise, we are moving and shifting the energy field, and by doing so, we are creating a freer flow. We all know the "feel good" state of mind we achieve by doing that.

2. The problem is that we tend to repeat the same sequence of exercises which means the same pattern of moving. Mostly, these follow a certain structure like running, Pilates, yoga, weight lifting, etc; these are all good, but they are missing an exploration of personal and spontaneous expression of the body. It is important to add to your exercise routine a section where you explore and experiment with moving your body the way it wants to move and/or moving your body in agreement with the feelings that you have at that moment.

3. Start with this exploration by putting on some music that you like and in the privacy of your home, or even in an empty and available room in the gym. Start moving as if no one is looking, just for fun. Try new moves, play, be silly, even ridiculous and let your body tell you how it wants to move. See if you can learn to follow your body rather than dictate to it how to move. There is a whole new world that can be revealed to you through this exploration. You might encounter feelings, or you might be flooded by images. You might find yourself reverting to your joyous, silly five-year-old self, or you might find your sexy, rebellious adolescent. Give yourself the chance to discover your body and yourself.

LET THE HEART SPEAK

Reflect on the last time you allowed yourself to move and dance spontaneously. How did it make you feel? When other people are around you who are doing this – abandoning themselves into dance – how did that make you feel?

If you haven't done this type of dance movement for some time or never, why is that? How can you encourage yourself to do it?

WRITING REFLECTION

_____

_____

_____

Use Your Body To Tap Into Emotions In Your Daily Life

Your body stores within its cells and DNA your experiences, your beliefs, desires, and needs. If you are passionate about growth, personal power, and transformation, you must learn to listen to your body and work with it.

One of my clients noticed that whenever she was angry, she literally felt the anger in her upper arms—an uncomfortable pressure within them causing them to ache. To relieve this sensation, we experimented with movements and sounds using her arms—punching the air, and letting her body move authentically in a way that felt natural to her, channeling this expression of the anger through physical movement so we could release it. It might have looked strange to an observer, but the results were tangible. Once she had released some of the anger through this exercise, she was able to contact the deeper layers of need and pain that were hiding behind the anger. With these emotions uncovered, she and I could find creative, productive ways for her to fulfill her needs and ease her pain.

One of the ways she was able to move forward after these sessions was by opening a path of communication and asserting herself.

This client was struggling in a business relationship with a partner who was negative and doubting, and the client needed a healthier, more positive atmosphere to make the business and the partnership work. Tapping into this need, she was able to assert herself with her business partner, established better work dynamics, and overcome a source of stress in her daily life.

Now, please take a minute to reflect and go through the following exercise.

LET THE HEART SPEAK

Exercise:

1. Take a moment to listen to your body and feel: Where are you storing tension at this moment? The tension may be in your jaw, your shoulders, your lower back, your stomach, etc. Feel it out and pinpoint it.

2. Sitting silently, touch the area on your body that is the location of this tension.

3. Take a few deep breaths imagining the air moving through that part of your body, in and out.

4. Ask yourself: What are the feelings that I am storing in this part of my body at this moment? Allow yourself intuitively to guess these feelings. Maybe you have a knot in your stomach because you are upset about a conversation with your friend, or your boss. Maybe you have tension in your back and shoulders from stressing over your finances.

5. Acknowledge the feeling. Accept it. Meditate on ways to relieve or attend to these feelings.

6. Take action. If you are worried about your finances, ask yourself what you can do to address the issue. Do something for yourself that is productive and nurturing to help you with that feeling. Don't avoid it or try to run away from it.

WRITING REFLECTION

_____

_____

_____

The Gate Of Emotions

Can you imagine your life without the presence of feelings in it?

All the magical and painful moments that infuse life with moving depth and richness will not exist. The fire and passion, as well as the stillness of awe, the sweetness of prayer, the inspiration of beauty, the depth of love and the fleeting fragrance of bliss will all be gone. Feelings are life's elixir; the most precious gift we have.

The heart, home of our emotions, is innocent and direct. When it is open, it is a fountain of love and joy, a generator of bliss, playfulness and creative impulses. When the heart is closed, caged, and repressed, our life force is blocked. We are not breathing, emotionally speaking. Thus, we are not fully alive- we just exist. The heart is also the master of our physical reality; it conducts the music that is the energy of our being. All physical manifestations are informed and effected by our feelings. If we are committed to being emotionally alive and physically healthy, we must recover and release the heart so it can return to its open and magical nature.

Allow yourself to feel daily. Gently surrender, accept and enjoy your feelings, even the painful ones. Experience the beauty and power that comes from being emotionally alive.

WRITING REFLECTION

_____

_____

_____

Getting To Know Our Emotional Self

One of the ways to find out about your emotions is to visit them regularly. Pay attention to them when they surface, listen carefully, and write down a few lines about specific emotions that moved you. Taking the time to acknowledge emotions is a way of respecting them. Respect leads to understanding and acceptance. Emotions that are understood and accepted can move freely.

There is a guided visualization I often use with clients, that helps to uncover the secrets of our emotional self. It is called "Visiting the Home of Your Feelings." The home of your feelings is a place within you (in your Emotional-Self) where all your experiences and emotions live. It contains many "rooms," and each one encompasses landscapes, images, colors, people, object, as well as bits of memories, smells, sounds, and words. Each room is never quite the same whenever you visit it. It continues to unfold, and every visit takes you to new and familiar realms. There is the room for fear, the room for pain, the room for needs, the room for peace, the room for sexuality, the room for loneliness, the room for adventure, and so on. As you can see, it is a vast home.

When I use this visualization, I always suggest to clients to visit one specific room at a time, and to choose the one they feel they need to visit most at the time of the exercise. They are always surprised by what is revealed when they enter the room they chose. Below are the guidelines for this exercise if you wish to do it at home by yourself.

Exercise- Visiting the "Home of Your Feelings."

GETTING TO KNOW OUR EMOTIONAL SELF

1. Lie down on your back in a comfortable position. Make sure that you will not be interrupted for the next half-hour to 45-minutes.

2. Start with a general relaxation. First, work to relax your body and all of its parts. Then, relax your mind by suggesting to yourself that it is time to drop thoughts and create stillness. Then bring your attention to your breath. Begin to follow your breath as you breathe in and out.

3. Once you feel you are relaxed, imagine walking on a tree-lined wide country road. It is a sunny day and you are walking to the home of your feelings. After a minute or two of imaginary walking, notice the home of your feelings from afar, at the end of the road. These images should come to you easy, directly, and spontaneously. Trust whatever comes up first!

4. As you approach the home of your feelings, notice, what it is made of, where it is located, and what is around it. Allow yourself to see as many details as possible: the colors of the walls, the surroundings, the path leading to the front door and any objects around the home.

5. See yourself coming down the path, approaching the front door and opening it. Notice if the door is locked or not. If it is locked, do you have the key? Once inside the home, notice the general feeling in it. Is it a pleasant, open, and a lit environment? Or is it dark, brooding, dusty, or mysterious? Are there windows? Is there a basement or an attic? Are there staircases leading to anywhere?

6. As you are walking around the house, pick a room that you want to visit, one connected to the theme you have been working with. Search the house to find this room. It may be in the basement, on the top floor or down the hall. For example, you may choose

the room of self-doubt, the room of shame, or maybe the room of love and intimacy.

7. Once you have found this room, the room that would deepen your understanding about the feeling that you have chosen, open the door to the room and step in. Take a minute to discover what is in the room. Do you see people? Who are they? What objects are there? Or is the room empty? What's the feeling that you have when you stand in that room? The next few moments are exceptionally important. If you allow yourself to experience whatever happens in this room, you will discover something new and important about this emotional place. Sometimes, emotions that are repressed come to the surface. Memories can come up, imaginary figures may show their faces, and the voices and sounds of your emotional past and future will come to you. Your subconscious is bringing forth images, symbols, and feelings, much like being in the dream state. Hence, do not control it. Allow the experiences to flow as they may. Most of the time, the journey has a natural beginning, middle, and end. A sense of clarity and relief follows.

8. Once you have completed the process in the room, it will be time to say goodbye to it. Bear in mind, that you may want to visit the room a few more times; saying goodbye means "see you later." Come out of the room, walk to the front door, step out of the house, and begin to walk back to the country road that has taken you here—back into your actual reality.

This is a guided visualization; however, it can be done without guidance. Feel free to experiment with it as an emotional meditation and follow the steps in the guidelines. Let go of intellectualizations, expectations (about results and contents of the exercise), and preconceived notions. Allow yourself to be surprised, and at the end of the exercise, take a minute to write down your thoughts.

WRITING REFLECTION

The Inner Map

Based on our experience, repressed or not, we form interpretations, memories, belief systems, patterns of behavior, and expectations. Ultimately, we create our view of the past, our reality in the present, and our future. We can call the internal canvass of our assumed reality the "Inner Map." By that I mean, the total body-mind way of experiencing and interacting with self and life. The "Inner Map" affects our experiential lenses through which we see, feel, and interact with reality.

The purpose of our inner transformation work is to re-organize our inner map in such a way that we can experience the abundance, creativity, and joy that are available to us. Gates of Power® Method provides the tools to achieve this kind of inner transformation.

WRITING REFLECTION

_____

_____

_____

A Note On Nurturing

Many times we find ourselves upset about something, but we don't take the time to acknowledge our feelings and give ourselves the nurturing we need.

We sweep the feeling away by moving on to an activity, or we tell ourselves that it's "babyish" to feel that way. It might even scare us to "go there," and therefore we repress or deny the feeling.

When we don't take a minute to acknowledge and honor our feelings, it is as if we are telling ourselves that we don't deserve love and care. In this way, we are sending ourselves a message – a strong one. Our Emotional Self feels unheard and neglected. By doing this, we are repeating a pattern of neglect and rejection that we have carried within ourselves from childhood.

The art of self-nurturing is worth cultivating.

WRITING REFLECTION

_____

_____

_____

The Wounded Heart

Being human and alive is quite risky. The possibilities of being hurt, disappointed, and devastated wait around every corner. The probability of growing up bent out of shape is undeniable. Our hearts will not escape the wounds caused by living. We are lucky to possess the capability for awareness, the build-in urge for growth and the innate blueprint of wholeness. Our mind-body system has a blueprint which requires it to be in balance and harmony if it is to function correctly, hence the tendency to maintain wholeness. Our system also exhibits a strong sense of survival, which means any intense feelings that threaten our emotional and physical survival will be repressed, split and encapsulated automatically, in order to keep them out of our consciousness.

The two tendencies complement each other: survival and wholeness. We need both to grow and thrive. The twist is this: emotions that were buried mostly in early stages of life for the sake of survival later become the very threat to our survival. This is where survival and wholeness clash. Repressed emotions generate a tremendous amount of stress and anxiety in our system. They short-circuit our energy field, creating pockets of disconnected tissue. They cause fragmentation within us and disconnection between us and the world. This creates a fertile ground for physical and mental diseases. So what are we to do? We must survive first, but then we shouldn't remain in survival mode; we need to move forward and integrate ourselves back into wholeness.

WRITING REFLECTION

_____

_____

_____

The Power Jog! Try This!

Gates of Power Method teaches you to nurture yourself—mind, body and spirit. Let's take the "Gate of the Body" and examine how we can better nurture and strengthen our bodies.

Step 1: Take an inventory of your daily patterns in the areas of nutrition (food and drink), exercise, rest (how do you sleep at night?), and grooming.

Step 2: Review the inventory of your daily patterns. Choose one area you would like to improve on.

Step 3: List three improvements you would like to make in your chosen area. For example, maybe you chose to improve your nutrition. So perhaps now you will drink more water, eat three square meals per day, and increase you intake of fresh fruit and veggies.

Step 4: Make a commitment to yourself in writing. For example, if your plan is to take water with you everywhere you go, jot this down as a plan of action. Do this for all three of your chosen improvements.

Step 5: Maintain a log for the next three weeks, detailing your strides and difficulties in improving your chosen pattern

At the end of the three weeks, give yourself a pat on the back for your accomplishment! Decide on how you would like to continue to improve your self-nurturing patterns by going back through your list and choosing another area to grow. Continue to record your progress in your log. Check back every three weeks to examine your activities.

You will see great change and results!

WRITING REFLECTION

_____

_____

_____

Magic and Miracles

Creating Magic

I went to see the movie, *Fantastic Beasts and Where to Find Them*. Needless to say, the child in me is fascinated by fantastic creatures and imaginary worlds. I could revel in these for hours; I love moving from on reality to another, mixing and matching the seen and unseen…

What really stayed with me after the movie, when I shook off the special visual and sound effects (which were a bit much to my taste) was the truth that we all possess magic powers and the ability to see and feel the magic within life. It is when we repress that ability or allow others to repress it in us that we become destructive to ourselves and others.

The magical power to create reality is our birthright and gift. It is what allows us to express and share with others. We can say that it is our spiritual air. Most of us, including myself, grew up, forced to repress our true power and expression for the sake of being accepted, loved, or safe. Many die with their inner music never fully sung. Others like myself, spend a chunk of life claiming back our magical powers.

Most of the time, the repression of our powers go unrecognized. We are so used to it, so it feels natural to us. So how do we know if we're operating from our power? Good question. Ask yourself, "Am I living life like it is a field of endless possibilities? Do I feel like I can manifest a vision that springs from my heart's passion into reality?" Openness to possibilities and a deep trust in our ability to manifest our desires is the state of mind where magic lives.

We need to recognize how we're in the way of our own magical powers. Fears, insecurities, distrust, self-doubt, etc. all are in the way. What are you doing to clear your path to true power?

WRITING REFLECTION

You Create The Miracles

Do you believe you can create miracles? Each one of us has at one point prayed and longed for a miracle. What's their secret? Where do they come from? Interestingly enough, the origin of Chanukah, the festival of lights, also depicts the origin of miracles. The holiday celebrates one of the grandest miracles in the history of Judaism. In 174 BCE, the Greek/Syrian Empire was occupying Israel and the neighboring region. In an attempt to strengthen and unify all parts of the empire, Antiochus, the Syrian/Greek Emperor, went on a rampage aiming to obliterate Judaism. A small band of Jews, at the beginning, there were only 12 of them, rose up and went to war against an enormous Greek army. They fought guerrilla style for three years, often amongst their homes and people. Many times, they felt like giving up, but they knew they couldn't. Their confidence in God was stronger than their admittance of defeat. It paid off, for after many years of bloodshed and against all the odds, they won.

It was a military, or should we say, a spiritual miracle. It showed us that miracles are the universe connecting with a soul that acts with conviction. For a miracle to occur, we must fully believe in what we are acting on. We have to come from a state of being in which we're willing to do everything it takes to uphold what we believe in; where giving up is not an option. Miracles won't come if you're waiting for them; they're gifts of your devotion. Only when we feel, believe, act fully and completely, can we create a miracle.

With this, I ask you, is there anything in your life that you're willing to give yourself up to completely? Do you have something you feel so strongly about that you could create a miracle?

WRITING REFLECTION

Halloween-Soul Magic

One of my deepest desires is experiencing life totally and unconditionally. I've been soul-searching for the secret of life ever since I was a young adult. My travels through the shadows and lights of living gave me the guidelines for living fully. Here are some:

1. Refrain from judging as much as possible. Judging keeps your heart closed.//
2. Stay authentic and vulnerable.
3. Accept all your feelings.
4. Speak your truth.
5. Embrace all parts of yourself: the clumsy, quirky, crazy, passionate, driven, and peaceful, etc.
6. Experience all parts of yourself.

This last one ushered me to audition for the Academy of the Performing Arts in Israel. Being an actor meant being a queen in one production, an orphan beggar in the next, a murderer in the third, and so on. Since being a character means finding it within you, I loved claiming all these parts of myself and embracing them. It took me awhile to discover that I am everything and everybody. We all experience murderous rage, intense loving devotion, tension, peace, hate, passion. The trick is to allow these energies to flow through us, to acknowledge them and listen to the needs hidden within their folds. We don't have to act out in response to all our emotions, but experiencing them fully allows us to open up to life.

I love Halloween. For a day, you have permission to be anything you are; a moment to taste the horrifying and magical, beauty and beast; a time to embrace the mystery of being alive.

We don't need Halloween's permission to accept every aspect of us. We're a sum of our parts; we can't be whole without embracing every little bit of us. With that, I ask you, what parts of yourself are you avoiding?

WRITING REFLECTION

_____

_____

_____

Co-Creating Your Reality

Believe it or not, you are co-creating your reality every single minute of your day. Your emotions and thoughts lead to actions and expressions that have tangible manifestations. We are energy and vibrations. Our emotions, thoughts and actions emit them. Who we are energy-wise attracts, repels, and shapes the energy around us. We begin tuning our vibrational instrument by intending to become an open channel of love, creativity, compassion, and joy.

Our commitment to that intention continues to take us back to the tuning. It's not just focusing on the positive; it's focusing on the truth. The truth is that in being one with the universal consciousness and energy, we are naturally made of loving compassion, joy, and creativity. Our intention helps us remember, realize, and actualize who we essentially and innately are. Asking ourselves "Who am I," helps us remember that we're not our fears, insecurities, and defensive habits.

Every time I ask this question in a workshop (and I have done this many times,) the answers that I hear from participants, both young and old, are similar. They say, "I am a creative, loving being." When I ask the second question, "Why are you here," (another one I've asked many times,) the answers are to "love, to learn, to grow, to create, to contribute." I ask them this so that in their quiet moments, my participants know who they are and why they are here. We need to learn to live in and identify with the part of ourselves that I call, the Expanded Self. It's not an easy task. Our Emotional and Defensive selves will pull us out of alignment. The sacred practice is to keep coaching, guiding, and healing these parts of ourselves so they can realign themselves with our Expanded Self. They will thus be assisting us in being, expressing, and acting from our true essence of love, creativity, and joy.

WRITING REFLECTION

The Power Of Intention

Intention is the generator of every creation.

Intention is a deep, heartfelt passion that lives within us, a true desire. When we are passionate about something, we naturally focus our thoughts and feelings on that subject. Our focus generates energy. This marriage of passion and focus is the creative power that fulfills our needs; whether from money, relationships, spiritual awakening, or love. Intention is the root of all motivation. Everything that happens in the universe begins with intention. Whether we decide to buy a gift, dance, or reach out to a friend, it all starts with intention.

The sages in India observed that our destiny is ultimately shaped by our deepest desires and intentions. In other words, as your desire is, so is your intention. As your intention is, so is your will. As your will is, so is your deed. As your deed is, so is your destiny.

An intention contains the seed of that which you aim to create. When you release your intentions with a sense of trust, into the depth of your consciousness, they grow and flourish. A natural path of choices, commitments, and actions springs out of your intentions. A consistent focus on your path will help you reach your destination.

WRITING REFLECTION

_____

_____

_____

On Creativity
An excerpt from the book, "Gates of Power: Actualize Your True Self"

I remember myself at 13 years of age, standing in one of these big aquariums; I believe it was in Eilat, a town by the Red Sea in Israel. I was awestruck by the endless colors, shapes, and variety of sea creatures floating in front of my amazed eyes. I recall thinking:

How could God come up with so many variations of fish? How could He [God was a He at that point in my life] invent so many shapes and colors? Where does He get all these ideas? He must be unbelievably creative. I wish I could have one-quarter of his talent.

Later, I started noticing the endless shades of yellow, gold, red, and brown painted on the falling leaves. I began noticing faces of people and shapes of clouds. I kept being amazed at God's talent and creativity. Some years later, I started to suspect that a little bit of this talent for the creative lived within me, a gift I was supposed to cherish and cultivate. Maybe, I thought, "This is my way of playing with God and creating for Him." It was fun to create, and I liked to imagine that it was making Him smile with pleasure.

The young version of myself got it right. The Great Creator loves creating, and we love creating *for* Him/Her and *with* Him/Her. When we create, we are in a dialogue with universal energy. We are realigning and transcending our limited notions. We expand. We dip into the mystery. We discover the unexpected. We find our wings. You are creative; we all are. Take yourself by the hand and commit to a creative way of being. You will instantly feel more excited about living- maybe a little scared, puzzled or doubtful, but tickled and curious.

WRITING REFLECTION

Shivaratri:
Constructive Destruction

On Friday night, February 28th, I participated in the Shivaratri celebration at Ananda Ashram. It was an all-night music and performance event celebrating Lord Shiva. I found myself bathing in the colors, the sounds, and the joy around me. I melted into a long meditation, surrounded by the rich vibrations of raga songs.

You might ask yourself, what does that have to do with you or me? Well, Shiva is the third god in the Hindu triumvirate. The three gods who are responsible for the creation, maintenance, and destruction of the world are Brahma the creator, Vishnu the preserver, and Shiva the destroyer. Shiva's role is to dissolve old patterns in order to facilitate re-creation.

We all are the creators of our life and the maintainers of it – hopefully in a responsible manner. We should also be able to dissolve old habits, patterns, and ways of being that do not serve us any longer, so that we can re-create our life anew over and over again. This is what Shiva has to offer us: the understanding that unless the old and unfitting is dissolved, the new cannot be created.

Hindus believe that Shiva's power of destruction and recreation are used to destroy the illusions and imperfections of this world, paving the way for beneficial change. This destruction is not arbitrary, but constructive. You might ask yourself, what are you holding onto that is illusory, impractical, and untrue? Wouldn't you want to be fierce and passionate like Shiva and find the courage to let go, release, and dissolve what is not essential or true within your life?

It is part of human nature to hold onto things as unbeneficial as they may be. We hold onto pain, insecurities, fears, people, things, untrue notions, and beliefs. The Shiva aspect within us – the courage to allow for the dissolution of obstructions – inspires a forward movement, a flow of continuous expansion and growth.

WRITING REFLECTION

_____

_____

_____

What Matters?

Last Saturday, I participated in a presentation by a good friend of mine, Lana Yu, an artist who lives in Peekskill. She had created a beautiful, big mural of public art that was going to hang on an outside wall of one of the buildings in Peekskill. It is called "What Matters?" Lana engaged many people from all walks of life - young, old, of different cultures, and of different backgrounds – and asked each one to write down what matters to them most. Many also participated in the actual painting of the mural. Doing so, Lana brought the community together. She was a catalyst, moving people to define what was most meaningful to them.

When invited to write what mattered most to me, I wrote "inner freedom." For, I believe when you are free on the inside, then you are truly able to love, to share, to contribute, to express, create, and so on. My personal journey was one dedicated to inner liberation. I walked a path of many shedding myself, again and again, releasing fears, anger, grief, and old confining beliefs. I feel I've shed lifetimes of soul weight. It brought me here with the ability to celebrate being me, being here, being one with all life, and just being. When it came to helping with the painting of the mural, Lana assigned me to paint somebody else's sentence, "Getting up in the morning." I had to smile. It was as if the angels decided to remind me to be grateful for just being able to get up in the morning so that I can enjoy my freedom and keep moving on the path.

What is most important to you? What gives your life meaning? What is your journey about?

WRITING REFLECTION

_____

_____

_____

Naked Trees, Unity, And Hope

I live by the park in New York City, and one of my small pleasures is taking a walking meditation in the park. Many insights, emotions and magic moments unravel themselves to me while walking in this urban sanctuary of nature. The other day, I was admiring the shapes of the naked trees, how vulnerable they looked and so expressive in their nakedness. They were bare, and at the same time, they looked strong in spite of their fragility. I thought about my journey to becoming stronger as I allowed myself to be more vulnerable, emotional, and authentic.

Real strength comes from our ability to reveal our inner truth, and that means vulnerability as much as conviction, passion, or assertion. So why are so many of us hiding behind a mask repressing feelings and covering our truth? Masks are divisive. When people hide from themselves, they hide from each other. As a result, they judge and distrust each other, and many times end up fighting each other. There is no unity when we pretend to be what we are not. We are always on guard, defensive, afraid to lose face, power or control. Without unity, there is no strength within or without. Families, cultures, and communities that can unite, survive crises much better than ones that are divided.

It is disturbing to observe our government unable to unite on crucial issues. People are internally divided, turning against each other, nations and religions unable to accept and embrace diversity. The President spoke in his inauguration speech about hope. Hope is an empty word without the sense of unity. We all share ONE ENERGY, literally and scientifically. We are all connected by similar basic human needs and desires. We are interrelated and interdependent, branches of the same tree. What would it take for us to realize this basic truth?

WRITING REFLECTION

_____

_____

_____

A Violin Out Of Trash

As I was sitting at my desk, I came across an email that a friend sent me about a documentary on a group of musicians in Paraguay. I learned that these musicians create their musical instruments out of pieces of trash. The symbolic meaning of this hit me. I thought about my last section that touched on the question: how much of our regular daily life are we <u>building or destroying</u>? Whether it is our small or big choices, our simple or grand actions, or our thoughts and feelings, all of these can either enhance this life, this world, or deplete it. Are we conscious of our impact?

Some of us enjoy resources, riches and available material, and what we do is take them and create destruction. For example, accumulation of wealth can be demonstrated by the purchase of expensive jewelry and diamonds; yet digging for diamonds often leaves natural resources and landscapes in shambles and devastation.

Others have very little resources, but are creating art, crafts, or adding in some practical way to the fabric of life like the musicians in the documentary, <u>*Landfill Harmonic*</u>. The choices we make, and how often we are conscious of them, can have a far-reaching impact on the world and others.

WRITING REFLECTION

_____

_____

_____

Winning The Inner Oscar

We love watching the Oscars. The beauty of the stars, the glamor of the gowns, the lights, the glitter, the entertainment and the artistic excellence all touch our hearts. They make us smile and might even turn us a bit green with envy. We, too, want to feel glamorous and admired.

Well, we truly desire such. If we could turn our eyes inward and catch a glimpse of our glorious spirit, we would be awed and amazed.

The same consciousness that created the rivers, the stars, the mountains and all the galaxies resides within us. It shines through our smiles, loves through our energy and creates.

Look within you.

Beauty, excellence, and love are your true essence. If only you could just know it, feel it and enjoy it, you would realize the star that you really are and the contribution you make by being yourself.

WRITING REFLECTION

_____

_____

_____

Healing: How Does It Happen?

As I was walking in the park the other day, I noticed a beautiful tree with a long broken branch lying on the ground next to it. "Does the tree feel it is broken?" I heard my Emotional Self ask, almost aloud. "I think it does," I responded. "But it knows how to grow new branches, so it is probably not so sad." "Ah," said my Emotional Self relieved.

Have you ever felt broken? I have many times. How did you deal with it? How do we heal from a broken heart, a loss of a loved one, loss of health, or broken dreams? From where do we draw the strength to heal?

The art of healing comes from nature. Nature, or cosmic consciousness, has given us the gift of healing. It is implanted within our psyche and physical body. What helps us activate this healing ability is love. Love starts with oneself. Self-love means, aside other things, a willingness to look inside, see the source of our pain, and have the courage to deal with it. Self-love is also a dedication to openness, acceptance, and communication. All these allow our emotions, thoughts, and energy to have a free healthy flow. Healing happens when an organic flow is maintained.

The secret of health for both mind and body is not to mourn for the past, worry about the future, or anticipate troubles, but to live in the present moment wisely and earnestly.

Buddha

WRITING REFLECTION

_____

_____

_____

Express Your Feelings By Using The Arts

We can think of feelings as currents of energy or currents of water. When currents are flowing unblocked, they maintain their natural rhythm and integrity. It's the same with feelings. When they are allowed to flow freely, they maintain their holistic nature. Using the Arts is a great way to keep our feelings in a state of flow and constructive expression.

We all know how music allows us to bask in the state of our feelings. Those feelings can be both positive and negative. If you are experiencing or have experienced negative feelings, it's important to know that you do not have to get stuck there – you can release them. If on the other hand, you are experiencing positive feelings, learn to celebrate and embrace them. The Arts are a great way to do that.

I would like to suggest using art-making, like drawing, or coloring, as part of your daily life. All it takes is a sketchpad and some crayons or markers. Keep them around the house and when you are aware that you have a feeling that you want to explore or express yourself, take some colors and put them on the pad. You're not a professional artist – and that's OK!

Allow your feelings to guide you, and don't think so much about what it is that you're doing. It's almost as if your heart pours into your hand – and then into the pad. You will be surprised how wonderful it feels and what you eventually produce.

LET THE HEART SPEAK

WRITING REFLECTION

_____

_____

_____

Author & The Gates Of Power® Program

Nomi Bachar, a holistic spiritual counselor, is a self-healing, self-actualization expert and coach. She is the director of White Cedar Institute for Expanded Living LLC and the creator of the Gates of Power ® Method.

The Gates of Power ® Method is a comprehensive curriculum that supports and maximizes the process of self-transformation and self-actualization, leading to empowerment. The curriculum includes seven levels that can be completed in three stages. The seven levels of the program build upon each other. Participants need to complete each level before moving to the next one. Each level includes discussions, interactive processes, and experiential exercises from each of the seven Gates.

To read more about The Gates of Power ® Method and its impact on self-development and growth, read Nomi Bachar's book, *"Gates of Power: Actualize Your True Self,"* which can be found on Amazon.com. For more information, visit www.gatesofpower.com.

CPSIA information can be obtained
at www.ICGtesting.com
Printed in the USA
LVOW07s1249190817
545627LV00001B/88/P